DATE DUE

Teens and Sex

OTHER BOOKS OF RELATED INTEREST

OPPOSING VIEWPOINTS SERIES

Abortion
Adoption
Human Sexuality
Sex
Teenage Pregnancy
Teenage Sexuality
Teens at Risk

CURRENT CONTROVERSIES SERIES

The Abortion Controversy
Teen Pregnancy and Parenting

AT ISSUE SERIES

The Ethics of Abortion
Sex Education
Teen Sex

DISCARDED

Teens and Sex

Myra H. Immell, *Book Editor*

Daniel Leone, *President*
Bonnie Szumski, *Publisher*
Scott Barbour, *Managing Editor*
Brenda Stalcup, *Series Editor*

Contemporary Issues
Companion

Greenhaven Press, Inc., San Diego, CA

Every effort has been made to trace the owners of copyrighted material. The articles in this volume may have been edited for content, length, and/or reading level. The titles have been changed to enhance the editorial purpose. Those interested in locating the original source will find the complete citation on the first page of each article.

No part of this book may be reproduced or used in any form or by any means, electrical, mechanical, or otherwise, including, but not limited to, photocopy, recording, or any information storage and retrieval system, without prior written permission from the publisher.

Library of Congress Cataloging-in-Publication Data

Teens and sex / Myra H. Immell, book editor.
    p. cm. — (Contemporary issues companion)
    Includes bibliographical references and index.
    ISBN 0-7377-0844-1 (pbk. : alk. paper) —
ISBN 0-7377-0845-X (lib. : alk. paper)
    1. Teenagers—Sexual behavior. I. Immell, Myra H. II. Series.

HQ27 .T434 2002
306.7'0835—dc21   2001040746

© 2002 by Greenhaven Press, Inc.
10911 Technology Place, San Diego, CA 92127

Printed in the U.S.A.

CONTENTS

FOREWORD

In the news, on the streets, and in neighborhoods, individuals are confronted with a variety of social problems. Such problems may affect people directly: A young woman may struggle with depression, suspect a friend of having bulimia, or watch a loved one battle cancer. And even the issues that do not directly affect her private life—such as religious cults, domestic violence, or legalized gambling—still impact the larger society in which she lives. Discovering and analyzing the complexities of issues that encompass communal and societal realms as well as the world of personal experience is a valuable educational goal in the modern world.

Effectively addressing social problems requires familiarity with a constantly changing stream of data. Becoming well informed about today's controversies is an intricate process that often involves reading myriad primary and secondary sources, analyzing political debates, weighing various experts' opinions—even listening to firsthand accounts of those directly affected by the issue. For students and general observers, this can be a daunting task because of the sheer volume of information available in books, periodicals, on the evening news, and on the Internet. Researching the consequences of legalized gambling, for example, might entail sifting through congressional testimony on gambling's societal effects, examining private studies on Indian gaming, perusing numerous websites devoted to Internet betting, and reading essays written by lottery winners as well as interviews with recovering compulsive gamblers. Obtaining valuable information can be time-consuming—since it often requires researchers to pore over numerous documents and commentaries before discovering a source relevant to their particular investigation.

Greenhaven's Contemporary Issues Companion series seeks to assist this process of research by providing readers with useful and pertinent information about today's complex issues. Each volume in this anthology series focuses on a topic of current interest, presenting informative and thought-provoking selections written from a wide variety of viewpoints. The readings selected by the editors include such diverse sources as personal accounts and case studies, pertinent factual and statistical articles, and relevant commentaries and overviews. This diversity of sources and views, found in every Contemporary Issues Companion, offers readers a broad perspective in one convenient volume.

In addition, each title in the Contemporary Issues Companion series is designed especially for young adults. The selections included in every volume are chosen for their accessibility and are expertly edited in consideration of both the reading and comprehension levels of the audience. The structure of the anthologies also enhances accessibility. An introductory essay places each issue in context and provides helpful facts such as historical background or current statistics and legislation that pertain to the topic. The chapters that follow organize the material and focus on specific aspects of the book's topic. Every essay is introduced by a brief summary of its main points and biographical information about the author. These summaries aid in comprehension and can also serve to direct readers to material of immediate interest and need. Finally, a comprehensive index allows readers to efficiently scan and locate content.

The Contemporary Issues Companion series is an ideal launching point for research on a particular topic. Each anthology in the series is composed of readings taken from an extensive gamut of resources, including periodicals, newspapers, books, government documents, the publications of private and public organizations, and Internet websites. In these volumes, readers will find factual support suitable for use in reports, debates, speeches, and research papers. The anthologies also facilitate further research, featuring a book and periodical bibliography and a list of organizations to contact for additional information.

A perfect resource for both students and the general reader, Greenhaven's Contemporary Issues Companion series is sure to be a valued source of current, readable information on social problems that interest young adults. It is the editors' hope that readers will find the Contemporary Issues Companion series useful as a starting point to formulate their own opinions about and answers to the complex issues of the present day.

INTRODUCTION

According to Teen Research Unlimited, a Chicago-based marketing research company, there were 31 million teenagers in the United States in 1999, and there will be more than 35 million by 2010. Most experts agree that in general these Generation Y teens are richer, more optimistic, more diverse ethnically and culturally, and smarter about modern technology than were the generations before them.

A CBS News poll that tracked more than 2,300 students across the United States through four years of high school confirmed Teen Research Unlimited's conclusions, and added a few others as well. Poll results showed that young people in the United States today are more jaded than their parents were when they were teenagers, more accepting of divorce, more familiar with handgun violence and drug abuse—and more sexually active. In fact, approximately 50 percent of the graduating seniors polled in 2000 said they had had sex (compared to 18 percent just two years earlier), and 18 percent said they were not virgins when they entered high school.

Other statistics confirm that teens are more sexually active today than in the past and that this early sexual activity is not unique to one ethnic group, one geographic area, or even one nation. The high rate of teenage sexual activity is very much an issue of concern in many parts of the world, including the United States. The statistics are sobering. For example, according to a report on teen sexual activity issued in August 2000 by the Henry J. Kaiser Family Foundation, in 1999 half of all U.S. students in grades nine through twelve had had sexual intercourse, and 8.3 percent had become sexually active before age thirteen. Numbers released shortly after by the Pennsylvania-based Center for Parent/Youth Understanding were even higher, indicating that seven out of ten girls and eight out of ten boys will have had sexual intercourse by the time they graduate from high school.

Given these statistics, it is not surprising that some adults assert that young people today are promiscuous. Many teenagers do not agree with this assertion, countering that adults judge them too harshly without considering the reasons why young people are more sexually active than they used to be. These teens point out that society has changed greatly over time—even during the last five or ten years—with respect to attitudes toward sex. For example, movies and television shows have become increasingly more graphic, and the underlying philosophy of most popular advertisements is "sex sells." In the words of high school student Michelle Boik, "Teens have not become more sexually active because they are 'bad' but because the situation is more obvious. . . . This does not excuse the pregnancy rates. But perhaps the change in what is considered appropriate or not appropriate in society could be the cause."

Obviously, when it comes to the risks and consequences of teen sexual behavior and activity, statistics do not necessarily tell the whole story. In fact, some recent statistics reveal that teen sexual activity may actually be decreasing. For example, a 2001 report issued by the federal National Council for Health Statistics indicated that the number of sexually experienced teens, which had increased steadily from the late 1980s to the early 1990s, leveled off in the mid-1990s. The report also noted that the pregnancy rate for girls between fifteen and nineteen has been declining steadily since 1991. Most Americans would agree that this data is encouraging. Yet despite these recent declines, the overall consequences of teen sexual behavior still invoke a disturbing reality. Consider these facts: The United States has the highest rate of teen pregnancy and births among the world's industrialized nations, and one in four sexually active teenagers will become infected with sexually transmitted diseases (STDs).

The high incidence of pregnancy and STDs among sexually active teens has led to increased interest in school-based sex education programs. Sexuality education has long been a topic of debate in the United States. In past decades, the primary issue of contention was not what material should be taught but whether sex education should be taught in school at all. Many adults felt strongly that sexuality education was the responsibility of parents and had no place in the schools. In recent years, however, the high rates of teen pregnancy and STDs in the United States have contributed to significant changes in attitude: Most adults no longer oppose sexuality education programs in schools. In fact, the majority of Americans are very much in favor of such programs. According to Debra Haffner, former president of the Sexuality Information and Education Council of the United States, "The question is never sexuality education yes or no. The question is whether it's left to chance or taught by trained teachers in a comprehensive program that covers a range of attitudes and skills that young people need." And therein lies the debate: Which message should sex education programs teach—safe sex or abstinence?

Although Americans have different opinions about teen sex, the majority believe that society should send a strong message to all teens that they should not have sex until they are out of high school. But the details of the message that these students receive depends in great part on the school they attend, the state they live in, and prevailing political views. Each school district follows its own guidelines concerning sex education, and these guidelines are often affected by state mandates or laws about what types of material can be covered in sex education classes. The most significant debate focuses on whether the curriculum should only stress abstinence or whether comprehensive information about sexuality and safe sex practices should also be included.

Some educators and other adults believe sex education programs

should present abstinence as the only option for teenagers. Abstinence-only programs typically teach that premarital sex is not acceptable morally, religiously, or socially; they also stress that contraception does not reliably prevent pregnancy or STDs. Supporters of the
abstinence-only approach argue that because teens are not prepared
for the consequences of sex, they risk both physical and psychological
harm if they engage in premarital intercourse. They contend information about safe sex should be excluded from the curriculum because it
encourages students to become sexually active before they are physically and emotionally prepared. "Even if you ignore the fact that
there are at least 25 active sexually transmitted diseases out there, and
even if you ignore teen pregnancy," states abstinence-only educator
Cathi Woods, "you can't take out the fact that every time you have
sex with someone and they leave you, there's a broken heart." According to Woods and other advocates of abstinence-only sex education,
teens need to hear that saving sex until marriage is the only option
that will ensure their safety and well-being.

On the other hand, many educators assert that while abstinence
until marriage is a valid part of sex education, it should be presented
merely as the safest option. To teach young people that abstinence is
the only option, they contend, is not a realistic approach in the current social climate. As college student and safe-sex advocate Jennifer
Schaum points out, presenting abstinence as the only option ignores
"the simple fact that lots of kids will, and do, have sex before they are
married." Critics of abstinence-only education maintain that it frequently avoids discussion of safe sexual practices that potentially
could prove life-saving to young people. This lack of knowledge could
be harmful to teenagers who decide to become sexually active without knowing how to protect themselves, these critics argue. As an
alternative, they promote sex education programs that have a more
comprehensive curriculum, including discussion both of the benefits
of delaying sexual activity and the proper use of contraceptives.
According to proponents of comprehensive sex education, the best
approach is to provide thorough and nonjudgmental information
about sexuality, STDs, pregnancy, and contraceptives.

The ongoing debate over what constitutes the most beneficial curriculum for sex education in the schools is just one of the topics covered in *Teens and Sex: Contemporary Issues Companion*. In the following
chapters, the authors examine relevant statistics and current trends in
adolescent sexual behavior. They candidly discuss gender identity
issues and the challenges confronting gay and lesbian teens in today's
society. The factors that contribute to the high teen pregnancy rate
are also explored, as is the alarming incidence of AIDS and other sexually transmitted diseases among adolescents. Taken as a whole, this
anthology provides a comprehensive and enlightening overview of
teen sexual behavior and its many ramifications.

CHAPTER 1

TEEN SEXUAL BEHAVIOR: AN OVERVIEW

Contemporary Issues
Companion

TEEN SEXUAL BEHAVIOR: MISCONCEPTIONS AND REALITIES

Sandra Kallio

In the following selection, Sandra Kallio focuses on the results of a national survey of thirteen- to seventeen-year-olds conducted by *Seventeen* magazine to determine teen attitudes and perceptions about sex. Kallio reports that there is a large discrepancy between teens' perception of the number of their peers who are having sexual intercourse and the actual number who admit to having had intercourse. In fact, she reveals, the majority of teens are not having sex until they are seventeen or older. Teens and experts alike believe that teens who have open and frank discussions with their parents about sex are less likely to become sexually active at an early age or with more than one partner, she writes. Kallio is the assistant features editor for the *Wisconsin State Journal.*

Seventeen magazine does not target parents of teens, but mom and dad could get a glimpse of their sons and daughters' world by reading the April 2000 cover story on "What You Think About Sex: Who does what, where and why? Our national poll."

It is, if nothing else, a starting point for conversations about . . .

- Perception and reality: 75 percent of teens think other teens are having sexual intercourse but just 40 percent say they've had intercourse.
- Oral sex: 45 percent say oral sex counts as sex, 40 percent say it doesn't and 15 percent aren't sure. However they categorize it, 55 percent of the youth ages 15 to 19 say they've engaged in oral sex.
- Contraception and protection: Of the teens who are sexually active, only 46 percent use condoms all the time.
- Homosexuality and experimentation: In a similar 1991 survey, 27 percent of the teens said "homosexuals have something wrong with them," compared to 19 percent in the 1999 survey. Of the teens surveyed in 1999, 15 percent say they have had a sexual experience with someone of the same sex.
- Talking about sex: Teens whose parents don't talk to them about

sex—21 percent of the teens surveyed—are more likely to take sexual risks, such has having sex younger and with multiple partners.

The firm that conducted the survey collected 1,105 questionnaires
from youth ages 13 to 19 at shopping malls nationwide; the results
were weighted to represent a national sample.

"We have information from several different surveys about the
number of teens who have engaged in intercourse by, say, age 17, but
not a lot ask about oral sex," said Monica Rodriguez, director of information and education for the New York–based Sexuality Information
and Education Council of the United States (SIECUS).

Forty percent of teens say they've had sexual intercourse, according
to the *Seventeen* national survey. . . .

The Role of Peer Pressure

Peer pressure was addressed in the *Seventeen* survey: 19 percent of boys
said peer pressure was their main influence for having sex, compared
with 9 percent of girls.

"That breaks my heart. I wish both responses to that were zero,"
says Rodriguez, adding that the number of teen-age boys feeling pres-
sured to have sex was frightening. "It speaks to why we need to be
doing this education. There is a misperception among young people
that more people are having sex than they are."

The reality, she said, is that most teens aren't having intercourse
until age 17 and up. "We need to tell them what the reality is, how to
deal with peer pressure and help them stick to their decisions."

Finding out not everyone is "doing it" can help teens, says Renee
Rostad, director of Lifewise, a nonprofit group founded by the Pregnancy Information Center in Madison, Wisconsin, to promote abstinence among youth. "That is very empowering to teen-agers. Especially on the girls' faces (at Lifewise programs), a light goes on and
they think, 'Wow, I don't have to do that.'"

The facts SIECUS presents in its 1995 publication "Facing Facts:
Sexual Health for America's Adolescents" include:
- The average age at first intercourse is 16 for males and 17 for
  females in the United States.
- The majority of teen-agers who have intercourse do so with
  someone whom they love or seriously date.
- Typically, teen-agers who have intercourse do so less than once
  a month.

Ongoing Open Dialogue Is Important

Those who are sexually active at a young age need to get complete
information about sexuality, Rodriguez said. "As this (*Seventeen*) survey shows, they're making all sorts of decisions about sexuality, and
not necessarily ones we as adults might agree with."

She also wants teens to understand that they can change their minds about sexual behavior.

"It's also important that young people understand that if they have engaged in sexual behavior in the past, they don't have to do it again," Rodriguez says. "Young people think once they do something that they can't ever say no to that behavior again."

A third of the teens surveyed by *Seventeen* magazine said they're not getting enough information from their parents on birth control or the biological and emotional aspects of sex.

Delivering The Big Talk is not enough, says Rodriguez, who advocates ongoing, open dialogue.

"It's never too late to talk to your kids about sexuality," Rodriguez says. "It's really important for parents to realize that kids do want to hear what their parents have to say about sexuality."

"From a Christian perspective, we teach abstinence," says Jackie Lee Colbert, who works with a group of about 30 youth ages 12 to 18 through her position as youth coordinator for Mount Zion Baptist Church in Madison, Wisconsin. "Our youth participate in the True Love Waits rally."

The year 2000 rally . . . featured games, music, speakers including Miss Wisconsin and teens signing a pledge that reads: "Believing that true love waits, I make a commitment to God, myself, my family, my friends, my future mate and my future children to be sexually abstinent from this day until the day I enter a biblical marriage relationship.". . .

Abstinence before marriage also is the main message of Lifewise. Rostad points out that the younger a person becomes sexually active, the more partners generally become involved and the greater the risk of emotional and health problems such as sexually transmitted diseases.

Pointers for Parents

Whatever a parent's message, Rodriguez, of SIECUS, offers guidance for getting started:

- First, decide what messages you want to give.
- Educate yourself so that you can answer questions and broach the subject of sex easier. "Sometimes parents feel their kids know more than they do, for example, about HIV because it was not taught in the past," Rodriguez says.
- If you feel uncomfortable talking about sex to your son or daughter, practice in your head or to a mirror. And remember, Rodriguez says, "It's OK to feel uncomfortable and it's OK for your kids to know this might be a little bit uncomfortable because that's reality." Your son or daughter already knows you're not perfect and will understand your message is so important that you're trying to overcome your discomfort to deliver it.
- Teachable moments happen not just for young children. The *Seventeen* survey could be one example to use in talking with teens about sexuality.

A Matter of Concern: Sex in Middle School

Anne Jarrell

In the following article, Anne Jarrell reports on the increase in sexual activity among younger teens and preteens. She explains that oral sex in particular has become a common phenomenon among young adolescents. According to Jarrell, young people today receive a very mixed message: They see explicit sex in magazines, in movies, and on television at the same time that they are being warned to stay abstinent until they are much older or married. Experts agree that this mixed message is the main reason for the higher incidence of sexual activity among middle-school students and younger youth, she states. Jarrell writes for the *New York Times.*

On the Upper West Side of New York City, Dr. Marsha Levy-Warren, a psychologist, said she is seeing more and more preteenagers who are going on junior versions of dates in fifth grade, at 10 or 11 years old. By seventh grade, they have graduated to sex.

"I can't tell you how many girls come in who are bereft about having had sex too soon," she said. "They went to a party, met a cute guy, he seemed to like them, they hooked up and did what they assumed everyone was doing. Then, they feel awful."

On the Upper East Side, Dr. Cynthia Pegler, a specialist in adolescent medicine, sees girls brought in by their mothers when they outgrow the pediatrician. These sophisticated young women may not be having intercourse at 13, but they are having oral sex. "They tell me oral sex is no big deal," Dr. Pegler said. "They don't see it as sex, but as safe and fun and a prelude to intercourse, where before, it used to be the other way around."

And in the suburbs, on Long Island, Dr. Wayne Warren, a psychologist, said groups of seventh and eighth graders rent limousines to take them to clubs in Manhattan, where they get drunk, grind on the dance floor and have oral sex in dim corners.

Teens Are Having Sex Earlier

In a society that is always pushing the envelope, the age at which sexual experimentation begins is speeding up, too, say psychotherapists, health professionals and school officials, who are concerned about the health and emotional ramifications for young teenagers.

"There are significant numbers of youngsters who are engaging in sexual activity at earlier ages," said Dr. Robert W. Blum, a physician and the director of the division of general pediatrics and adolescent health at the University of Minnesota, which analyzes data on teenage sexual activity for the federal government. "Besides intercourse, they are engaging in oral sex, mutual masturbation, nudity and exposure as precursors to intercourse."

In data published by Dr. Blum and his team in the *Journal of the American Medical Association* in 1997, 17 percent of a national sample of thousands of seventh and eighth graders had had intercourse. Other, smaller studies put the percentage even higher.

"I see no reason not to believe that soon a substantial number of youths will be having intercourse in the middle-school years," said Dr. Richard Gallagher, director of the Parenting Institute at New York University's Child Study Center. "It's already happening."

Sex Is Everywhere

Experts of all political and philosophical bents give many reasons for this phenomenon, including the rising divorce rate, inattentive parents, the availability of condoms and the earlier onset of puberty. But the most frequent explanation is that today's culture sends a very mixed message to its young.

On the one hand, bombarded by warnings about AIDS and sexually transmitted diseases, adolescents are taught abstinence, the sole contraception method taught at one-third of all public schools across the country, according to a recent poll by the Alan Guttmacher Institute, a private research organization.

On the other hand, teenagers are confronted daily with a culture that has become a very sexy place indeed in which to live. "Sex is everywhere, and it's absolutely explicit," said Dr. Allen Waltzman, a psychiatrist with practices on the Upper East Side and in Brooklyn, who sees many adolescents. "There's hardly a film that doesn't show a man and a woman having sex. There's MTV, lurid rap lyrics, and now we've got technosex on the Internet."

None of this is lost on young adolescents, Dr. Waltzman said. "Kids always push to the limit of what's permitted in a society."

Oral Sex Is Common

One 13-year-old boy at a junior high school in Manhattan said he first had oral sex at 12 and has had it about eight times at parties and in the hours between 4 P.M. and 7, before parents come home from work. The sex was never with a steady girlfriend, because he has never had one. "It's something to do with someone," he said. "I think it's curiosity. I don't think that's bad."

An eighth-grade private-school boy said that he and his friends know that oral sex "is not perfect," but that they believe there is less likelihood of picking up a sexually transmitted disease than with intercourse. "The schools tell us to refrain, they tell us you get STDs from both, but no one believes it," he said.

Dr. Warren, who practices in Manhattan as well as in Suffolk County, said: "Before, the dialogue was, 'I love you and care for you, so let's experiment.' Now, the dialogue is, 'This is safe and fun and OK, and you have nothing to worry about.'

"I see girls, seventh and eighth graders, even sixth graders, who tell me they're virgins, and they're going to wait to have intercourse until they meet the man they'll marry. But then they've had oral sex 50 or 60 times. It's like a goodnight kiss to them, how they say goodbye after a date."

Studies Focus on Older Teens

There are no in-depth studies showing national trends in sexual activity in middle school, ages 10 to 13. No one will finance such studies, Dr. Blum said, because of fear of the outcry from politicians who embrace an abstinence-only message and from parents wanting to protect their children's privacy.

The studies of national trends that do exist look only at high school students. These show a striking drop decade by decade in the age at which teenagers first engage in intercourse. A December 1999 study by the National Center on Addiction and Substance Abuse at Columbia University noted that in the early 1970s, less than 5 percent of 15-year-old girls and 20 percent of 15-year-old boys had engaged in sexual intercourse. By 1997, the figures were 38 percent for girls, 45 percent for boys.

In the wake of AIDS and of abstinence advocacy, statistics from the 1990s analyzed by the Guttmacher Institute show that the age by which a majority of teenagers had engaged in intercourse has not continued to fall. The teenage birthrate has been falling since 1991, in part, experts say, because of decreased sexual activity. (It is still the highest for the developed world.) The Centers for Disease Control and Prevention in Atlanta reports that among high school students of all ages, those who have had sex declined from 53 percent in 1995 to 48.4 percent in 1997, the latest year for which figures are available.

But Dr. Gallagher said that the apparent diminishing of high school sexual activity masks a more insidious development: some older teenagers may be extending their years of virginity, but some younger teenagers are having sex earlier.

"You can get 16- to 18-year-olds who will be very conservative sexually," Dr. Gallagher said. "And then you can get right below them a group of 14- to 16-year-olds who say those older students are too conservative, let's party."

A Timetable for Having Sex

Despite the paucity of data about young teenagers, educators say that the anecdotal evidence points to increased sexual activity, often of a detached, unemotional kind.

"The kids are overwhelmed with sexual messages, and we're seeing a younger and younger display of not only precocious sexual behavior but also aggressive sexual molestation, like holding down a student and forcibly pulling down his or her pants," said Dr. Frederick Kaeser, the director of health services for District 2 of the New York public school system, covering much of Manhattan.

"We do a terrible job of teaching sex education," he added.

One boy, 13, who attends a private school in Manhattan, said his interest in sex began in the third grade, watching *Beverly Hills 90210*, the television show that portrayed teenagers from well-off families in the boom economy behaving like adults. "I was interested," he said. "The people were cool. I wanted to try what they were doing on the show."

He, along with half a dozen of his friends, described a timetable for sexual initiation. By third grade, they knew the slang for activities from masturbation to oral sex. By fourth grade, they had girlfriends and were playing kissing games. By fifth, they were going on dates. In sixth, they were French kissing and petting. In seventh and eighth grades, they tried oral sex, and some had intercourse.

By ninth grade, one boy said, "it's just one big spree of going all the way."

The head of their school said she thought they were accurate in their timetable.

Asked if they felt things were going too fast, the boys shrugged. "It has to happen sooner or later," the 13-year-old said. "Sex is pleasurable. Why not now? Sometimes people get hurt. Sure. I've been hurt. But that's going to happen at any age."

Psychiatrists and psychologists, however, say that most young teenagers cannot handle the profound feelings that go with early sex. "Developmentally, they just aren't ready," Dr. Levy-Warren said. "They're trying to figure out who they are, and unlike adults who obsess first and then act, kids do the opposite—they act and then obsess. They jump into this, and are left with intense feelings they're unable to sort out."

What's most troubling to Dr. Levy-Warren and others is a new casual, brazen attitude about sex. "I call it body-part sex," she said. "The kids don't even look at each other. It's mechanical, dehumanizing. The fallout is that later in life they have trouble forming relation-ships. They're jaded."

While New York middle-school educators and counselors say they are increasingly concerned about earlier sexual activity, particularly oral sex, no one is clear on what to do about it. After Schools Chan-cellor Joseph A. Fernandez was fired in 1993, in part for introducing a condom-distribution program, the New York public schools have set-tled into a sex education curriculum that's a mixed bag of preaching, basic anatomy and, in high school, condom distribution, though par-ents can choose to keep their children from participating.

Even at New York's private schools, not concerned with federal guidelines, which since 1996 have allocated millions of dollars to sex education programs that teach only abstinence, ambivalence reigns. At Friends Seminary in downtown Manhattan, parents were called to a meeting in 1998 after students in a fifth grade class began pairing off and breaking up, and "the misery factor was high," said Pamela Wood, the head of the middle school. There was no consensus among the adults. Half were appalled at the prospect of 10-year-olds dating. The other half thought it was cute.

"In elementary school, everyone pretty much has the same agenda," Ms. Wood said. "By middle school, no one agrees on what is appropri-ate. As for parents, their egos can get entangled. They want their kids to be liked, and if dating is what it requires, then they're for it."

The sex education curriculum at Friends includes practice exercises in how to put on a condom for eighth graders and free condom distri-bution in high school, but there is disagreement about distributing condoms with fruit flavoring, for use during oral sex.

At the Dalton School on the Upper East Side, concern about the precocious sexual climate led to starting a sex education program for the fifth grade during the 1999–2000 school year, where none had existed so early before.

Dr. Glenn Stein, the middle-school psychologist, said that the pro-gram is mostly anatomy. "A little inoculation, I would call it," he said. "It's not enough, but it's a start."

What the fast-sex scene means to girls, as opposed to boys, is of particular concern to school psychologists, who mentioned holding discussions and seminars on gender issues. Deborah Tolman, a direc-tor at the Wellesley College Center for Research on Women, points out that anecdotal evidence indicates that when it comes to oral sex, "the boys are getting it, the girls no."

"It's the heterosexual script that entitles boys and disables girls," she said.

Discussion Needed Sooner

Most psychologists say that what is needed is not just to supply youngsters with facts and information about anatomy, but also to provide them with forums to explore their feelings and to digest the proliferation of sexual messages they receive. As Francesca Schwartz, a school psychologist at the Brearley School, a private school for girls on the Upper East Side, put it: "Do I really like this person? Or am I just doing this to be popular? These are the questions the kids need to learn to think about and ask."

Such discussions should come sooner rather than later, educators say. "Preteens in our culture are 8 and 9," said Dr. Ava L. Siegler, a psychologist and the author of *The Essential Guide to the New Adolescence.* "We shouldn't wait to talk to them about AIDS, sex and violence until they are 12."

Dr. Waltzman added: "To kids, their crushes and loves are the most important thing. Adults may see it as silly or irrelevant, but the kids don't. It does no good to leave them to figure it out on their own."

THE TEEN MINDSET ON SEX

Joan Atalbe

In the following selection, Joan Atalbe recounts a discussion with a group of Florida teenagers about their sex lives. These teens, writes Atalbe, believe that they are not as sheltered as their counterparts in the early 1990s; they acknowledge the need to practice safe sex and feel better-informed about sex overall. However, Atalbe explains that not all educators and other experts agree that young teens are well-informed about safe sex or that sexual activity among teens is on the decline due to fear of AIDS and sexually transmitted diseases (STDs). Atalbe is a writer for the *Sarasota Herald Tribune* in Sarasota, Florida.

They sat with watchful hesitation as the discussion of their sex life unfolded—not from embarrassment but from wonder that the topic turned on whether they practiced safe sex. It's a given as far as they're concerned.

Count that as the first difference between a 1999 sampling of South Florida teens and a similar dialogue with the same age group nearly a decade ago. Back then, students said they thought safe sex was something urged by adults to keep them from enjoying themselves. This time, no teen among some 50 students questioned believed that. Those quoted in this story typify others in the sampling.

A 15-year-old with choirboy looks, who just became sexually active this year, ignored the silence in a Lifestyles Skills class and said with deadly concentration, "I worry about AIDS, but I worry about pregnancy more. Unless you don't know about the person you're having sex with—like if they've been tested—it's OK. I use both birth control and safe sex, condom and oral birth control."

His fear of pregnancy is grounded in fact. According to the National Center for Health Statistics, a sexually active teen-ager who doesn't use contraception has a 90 percent chance of pregnancy within one year.

Which may account for the national statistic that about one in six teen-age girls practicing contraception combine two methods, primarily the condom with another method. The method that teen-age girls most frequently use is the pill (44 percent), followed by the condom

(38 percent). Another statistic shows that while nine in 10 sexually active girls and their partners use a contraceptive method, they don't always use it consistently or correctly.

"Like I didn't know until maybe four months ago or so that pre-cum could actually get you pregnant," said the 15-year-old, hooking one arm over the back of his chair. "I didn't know that. And people who have dry sex, like sex with your underwear on—I've done that when I was early 15—you know, I never thought . . . I mean I didn't actually have an orgasm, but pre-cum would come out and I didn't know that it could actually get somebody pregnant."

Explaining why illness is a secondary issue with him, the boy continued, "I use the same partner. I know that my partner has been with only one other person and that person was a virgin."

Unconvinced, a central-casting cheerleader with bouncy brown hair wondered if there's such a thing as safe sex.

"Having sex with a condom is not like 100 percent safe," she said. "Safer sex would be like he was talking about: having the girl on birth control, which is like 97 percent safe, and then also using a condom. Still safer than that would also be pulling out. So you're just limiting down with less sperm going in. But nothing is 100 percent."

One-third of teen-age women in the United States who rely on the condom use it either with withdrawal or the pill.

"It just takes one sperm," the girl went on to say. "So of course I wouldn't recommend as a protection just pulling out. Then there's that pre-cum, which is even before the cum that has sperm in it."

Another boy, Mr. Body-perfect, his arms folded tight as a gate, questioned the value of condoms in the first place. "I had a condom in my wallet," he said quietly, "had it in there for maybe a week, and it leaked. The heat in Florida, I guess."

The cheerleader also worried about leaking condoms.

"Another thing people are ignorant or stupid about is carrying a condom," she said. "I remember from some class I took that having it in your wallet, you can have safe sex. But even when he sits down and rubs against it, it can wear down. You don't know how old the condom is. So going out and having sex with a condom may make you think you're having safe sex, but the girl should have her own condom, because she's the one who's going to get pregnant."

Times Have Changed

Such cautionary words did not appear in a 1992 *Herald-Tribune* article on the mindset of teens on sex. In fact, the current breed, having read the article in advance of the discussion, laughed at it.

"Lots of the ideas in it were extremely humorous," said a bespectacled girl with porcelain looks. "The part about the grape jelly, I thought was extremely humorous, and the Coke part. That was just interesting."

She was referring to a girl who used a Coca Cola douche as a spermicide and another who believed that grape jelly can serve as a spermicidal jelly.

"I didn't know that people were actually—I don't want to say stupid or ignorant," the girl with the glasses went on to say. "I didn't realize that anybody ever thought that. I thought that most people like knew more than that. And that was still in the '90s."

"The sock," the cheerleader type said, and the room of 15 rocked with laughter. They were reacting to a section in the '92 story that recounted a TV message of a young man demonstrating the use of a condom by rolling a sock up his foot. The teens in '92 took the sock literally as a condom. It was one of the few times in the recent discussion that anyone even smiled.

"I think we're smarter now," said a tall, rangy boy, gazing into a private space. "The people who are having sex are starting younger, and I think it's really like scary, so the teachers are talking about it more, and it's more open. It's just not as sheltered. It's more out and everyone knows it and kids are doing it when they're 13, watching these TV shows and stuff. They start when they're like—some of them not even teen-agers yet, 12 years old."

More Opportunities for Information

Only three in this group of 15 acknowledged being sexually active. Two refrained from the head count, including the rangy boy. Counting the abstentions, the ratio of those abstaining from sex to those active was the same in discussions with other teen groups: One third were having regular intercourse.

The local count was not an isolated one. A report from the Alan Guttmacher Institute in April 1999 suggested that U.S. teens are more knowledgeable. Their pregnancy, birth and abortion rates have been declining since 1996. And the nationwide pregnancy rate for women ages 15 to 19 shows a 17 percent drop since peaking in 1990.

According to the report, sexual activity among young teens is down. Eight in 10 girls and seven in 10 boys are virgins at age 15. But there's a likelihood that young people will have intercourse in their mid-to-late teens. More than half of 17-year-olds have had intercourse.

Hilda Purvis, a 15-year veteran teacher in Lifestyles Skills in Sarasota, Florida, attributes the change in behavior to opportunities for information, gleaned not only from classes like hers, but from the numerous organizations that combine with classroom education to provide information.

For her classes, Purvis has gotten speakers from Coastal Recovery and the American Red Cross to talk about the HIV virus. She follows that up with guest speakers with AIDS.

"Students can also listen to news 24 hours a day, read newspapers on the subject and look up stuff on the Internet. And they've got friends who have had experience with AIDS, or abortion, unwanted pregnancy, all the venereal and sexually transmitted diseases. So they're getting it from all areas and they know it to be true. I think there is a healthy fear. I like the word 'healthy.' Sex is not something teens are rushing into blindly anymore."

Are the Studies Really Valid?

Lynn R. Bernstein, a licensed clinical psychologist in Port Charlotte, doesn't believe any of it.

"In my experience, there is no way that I could say that sexual activity is down. I deal with lots of girls and guys, and sex is the only way that their relationships work. And they're not practicing safe sex, either, especially girls. They want to keep the relationship. They don't want to engage in sex, but that's the thing to do. And boys say to them, 'Well, you're my first one, so you don't need protection because I don't have anything.'

"So I'm not sure how accurate it is to say right now that sexual activity is down. I have not come across the non-virgin," although she conceded that some virginity may exist.

How does Bernstein reconcile her clinical experience with national studies?

"Anonymous surveys, random samplings, what is the validity of their data? If you give out a piece of paper and say 'Fill this out,' kids are going to be sure you can trace their answer and they give the right answer. If you put it on computer, they'll answer it in the wildest way. If you go and ask them personally, you're an adult, they know what answers you want.

"It may be a badge of honor to be able to say, 'I'm the last holdout' or 'It's the moral values of my family or church, and I don't care if I never have any friends again. This is more important to me.' There are some of those kids. But I cannot say that it's a shared belief."

Bernstein also doesn't believe the finding that fear of AIDS and STDs drives teens from sex. Fear has never been a deterrent for any long-term behavior, such as smoking or criminal behavior, she said.

Bill Kinder, a professor of psychology at the University of South Florida specializing in human sexuality, both agrees and disagrees with Bernstein. He said that the data clearly show a decline in sexually active teens. But he agrees that fear tactics are not good ways to change behavior.

"Things like bringing AIDS patients with sores is reminiscent of the stuff in the early '60s when in phys-ed class, they'd show you gruesome films of cirrhotic livers from alcohol abuse and those kinds of scare tactics. That's probably not what's working with the teens."

But whatever it is, the good thing is that kids are thinking about safe sex, he said.

Purvis allowed that "there's a lot going on, but not as much as people think," she said. "I believe students are becoming more aware and choosing to wait. This doesn't mean they're going to be totally abstinent before marriage. But they're not entering relationships as early as once believed. If indeed they're telling the truth. But I think they don't have to lie."

Bernstein's not alone in thinking that teens may not be telling the whole truth. The mother of one of the high schoolers thinks teens are lying about abstaining.

"My mother doesn't believe I'm a virgin," said a girl in a breathy voice. "She thinks that everybody's doing it. I have a boyfriend and she doesn't see how somebody who is 18 years old can still be a virgin. I mean it's just such a stereotype that everybody's doing it that everybody thinks everybody is."

But a cherubic-faced girl, looking up with something fragile in her eyes, said, "I'm 16 now. I started to have sex when I was 15. I lost my virginity and my mother found out, so she put me on birth control pills. I've been with the same boy for a year and seven months. We use condoms and birth control pills. It's the safest way, because you can never tell if your boyfriend . . . I mean, you think he's faithful, but you really do not know if they're going to turn around and have sex with somebody else. Then you're sleeping with three different people that that person slept with and three different people that that person slept with. You don't know what you're getting."

"I'm waiting to have sex when I'm married because I don't want to be pregnant now," said a girl with a heavy Spanish accent. "I want to live my life before I get married to someone who cares, who stays with me and with the child being born and all. I just don't want a child and get all the stress because teen-agers now are getting too much stress from pregnancy, a child, abortion and all this stuff.

"I don't want to get pregnant, and I don't want to get sick, I don't want to lose my heart."

The cheerleader shook her bouncy hair in agreement.

"I think this in my head. What it is, you have a heart, and the more you date around and maybe sleep around, and like break your heart, and each guy that breaks your heart takes a piece of your heart. So you have sex with a guy and he takes a piece of your heart."

But a slight black girl with downcast eyes that never left her lap doesn't think it's realistic to expect teens to be celibate.

"With all the videos and movies out there with sex in them, it gets harder and harder not to have sex," she said. "And sometimes you can't help yourself. It happens. You meet somebody, you have sex with them. You're in the mood, you're going to do it."

"I'm saving myself for marriage, waiting for the right person," said an 18-year-old black senior in a starched button-down shirt. "I don't want to get sick," he said, his thumbs hitched in his belt. "I'm in a relationship right now, but we don't do anything, because I'm saving myself for the right person."

A FOURTEEN-YEAR-OLD MAKES THE BIG DECISION

Patricia Hersch

Patricia Hersch is a former contributing editor to Psychology Today. *Her articles have appeared in such newspapers and magazines as the* Washington Post *and* McCall's. *In the following excerpt from her book,* A Tribe Apart: A Journey into the Heart of American Adolescence, *Hersch describes fourteen-year-old Courtney's decision to lose her virginity. Courtney does not feel that she can talk to her mother or any other adult about sex or relationships, Hersch writes. She explains that Courtney's mother blames all of Courtney's unacceptable behaviors on peer influence and is unaware that the biggest issue in Courtney's life is whether or not to have sex with her current boyfriend. Hersch details Courtney's resulting confusion, her decision to have sex with her boyfriend, and the humiliation and loneliness she experiences afterward.*

Courtney is getting real tired of the male sex drive. First there was Brendon breaking up with her because she didn't want to do it just for fun. She likes to be close and to feel cared for like anybody else, but having sex—well, she remembers how she thought sex seemed like it might be cool when she was in seventh grade, but she isn't so sure now. She and her little middle school girlfriends, she recalls, were totally sex-crazed. Their attitude was, Ah, sex, let's try it. She recalls: "In seventh grade you know all the facts about it. You see TV and movies and you're like, Oh, we could have sex and get married and have children. It's a big fantasy. And you think it would be perfect. But you don't really think about the actual act of sex. You don't know how it's going to feel, or that you have to trust someone. You just think, He's a hot guy, let's have sex. And of course, in seventh grade, you don't really mean it."

Now that she is fourteen and a half and has a regular boyfriend, Nat, it could easily be real. Although scared and uncomfortable, she feels it is inevitable. . . .

Sharing Views on Sex

She met Nat through her best friend Dee. The end of the summer, the two girls were sharing a pizza when Nat came over to their table to say hello. Courtney knew who he was from her friends, but when he sat down and joined them, she had an opportunity to get acquainted herself.

That night, Courtney slept over at Dee's. She told her friend she thought Nat was cool and she'd like to see him again. She didn't have to wait long. The next afternoon, Nat met them at South Lakes Shopping Center, a popular hangout for young teens in Reston, Virginia. They sat around for hours by the lake talking. . . .

She was kind of shocked to find out that Nat was not a virgin. "I was surprised because Nat's a little guy, but he gets a lot of girlfriends. We all knew that. Most people at this age if they are having sex, then they'll just be really immature about it and brag. They just do it to just do it. It doesn't mean anything. They'll have sex with you and move on," says Courtney.

But Nat told her, "I wish I was still a virgin. It would be so much more meaningful." He said: "I don't understand why someone would want to have sex with someone and then leave them and not talk to them after. I would be just as happy with a relationship if all we did was kiss as I would be if we had sex all the time. I think if you have sex all the time then your relationship gets based only on sex."

Courtney thought Nat sounded so mature. . . .

The next day, while Courtney was baby-sitting, Nat called. This call blew Courtney away. "He told me that he liked me, and I thought that was good that he didn't go through friends like most people do. I thought that was mature of him to tell me himself." She told him she liked him too.

Parents May Be Fooled

The next morning, he walked all the way to her house so they could be together. They watched a movie and talked about how they liked each other. They sat awkwardly on the sofa in the family room and gradually worked their way toward each other, eyes glued to the television screen. He put his arm around her. She put her hand on his knee. It was a little uncomfortable but okay. Courtney kept telling herself to relax, that she was finally with somebody who knew what he was doing. . . .

By now, Nat had been at the house most of the day, a big no-no in the family rules. When Courtney's sister Ann heard their mom pull into the driveway after work, she alerted Nat and Courtney, who tore upstairs to the kitchen.

When her mom walked in, the two were leaning casually against the counter talking. Courtney introduced Nat and told her mom that he had only been there for half an hour. Ann lied for her. "Oh yeah, he just got here." Courtney's heart was doing flip-flops. She didn't think her mom was going to like him. "He looks like he would be some druggie because he's got long hair, he wears big clothes. He's not a very presentable-to-adults kind of kid, which I think is bad because I don't think adults should stereotype." She was certain her mom would size him up as a bad kid.

Her mom baffled her by being nice to Nat. She wasn't mean about him being there. . . .

Parents are rightfully confused. Who's a troublemaker and who is not is never clear anymore. "It's not like when we were kids," one mom laments. "There are no Greasers versus Preppie-types; there is no such thing as the clean-cut college type and the low-class dropout, certainly no rules for what 'nice' girls do or don't do."

Courtney's mother takes the time-honored position that the problems come from elsewhere, sweeping her daughter along. She goes on about all the bad influences around her daughter. . . . Her mother blames the kids who lack adult supervision, not understanding that all the calls to check in with her that she requires of Courtney and Ann are nothing but pro forma. . . .

Courtney has in no way been deterred from following her impulses. She still sees nothing wrong with being out in the middle of the night: "If we did what we did at two o'clock Saturday afternoon, then we'd be like, 'This is boring, this is really dumb.' But because it is in the middle of the night and we are the only people up, that's the only thing that makes it worth it." The middle of the night "is so much more laid back. You get to know people better." There is no hassle about having to ask your parents' permission but there are still rules: "Everybody knows we have to be home by four-thirty in the morning before parents get up." It is so easy to get away with because "it is not something parents think their children will do." . . .

Mixed Feelings Kept Hidden

Right from the start of their relationship, Courtney became aware of some odd things about Nat. In the manner of her generation, she doesn't judge him but she notices. He goes to a county school for the emotionally disturbed. She knows he sees a psychiatrist and is on medication. He's been hospitalized a few times for depression. But what's new about that? Lots of kids are in therapy.

Nat doesn't really go home, he just goes from one person's house to the next. He hates going home and Courtney doesn't know why. He comes from a large family but his older siblings are all grown. His parents don't get along but they are not divorced. His dad, who travels a lot, comes home about once every four months, "so they don't bother getting divorced," Nat told her. He likes his mom. She is nice to him and they get along, especially since she lets him do anything he wants. He says it is because "I have a bad temper and she's afraid that if she tells me what to do, I'll get mad at her and I'll like beat her up or something." . . .

While Courtney's mom lets down her guard a bit, accepting that Dee and Nat are nice kids, she is completely ignorant of the consuming issue in her daughter's life. Courtney is not thinking about doing drugs or how she'll do in school this fall. She's wrestling with the Big Decision about sex. . . .

At first Courtney is in seventh heaven. Nat is different because "most of the guys I go out with, I'm always the one who calls them, and I'm always the one who wants to see them." Nat calls her wherever she is and always stops by to visit. "Most people I have gone out with," she says, "say they like me but then don't really and it ends up being a two-week relationship." Nat is consistently nice and the relationship has gone on for a month.

She does have a little trouble with his devotion. He always wants to be with her. "He's like, 'I want to see you, I haven't seen you in a day.' I say, 'Can't you wait another day?' I'm nice about it, but it gets on my nerves sometimes." On the other hand, if she doesn't talk to him, she misses him. It's the same thing with kissing. Even though he always kisses her when they're around her friends, the first time they were alone he didn't. She doesn't understand herself. She's so nervous about things going too fast but when he didn't kiss her, she wanted him to.

Debating the Sex Decision

One night when Dee comes over, Courtney and she have their millionth discussion about sex. While the noise of the television drones in the background, they munch on M&M's and grapes. They go over the same ground as if it is new. Dee starts, "I haven't had sex yet, but hopefully I will love him."

"Yeah," says Courtney. "You've got to be sure they're smart enough to know about a girl's body."

"Right," says Dee. "You don't want to have sex with someone stupid."

"I told you I didn't know where this was leading with Nat," says Courtney with a sigh. "I don't know if it's going to lead to sex. I'm not sure."

"I think a lot of teenagers are stupid," says Dee, trying to make her friend's decision easier. "They think everyone's having sex so you have to too. A lot of people are having sex, but not that many. Personally, I don't think I'm mature enough to have sex anyway. I'm not comfortable enough with my body, let alone theirs, to have sex."

"The thing is," says Courtney, "I know I'd get so mad if I had sex with a guy and then they didn't speak to me again. I know I'd probably prefer them not to have sex with me at this stage in my life." She is ashamed of not wanting to have sex, thinking it shows how immature she is. She goes back and forth about Nat as her first partner. On the one hand, she thinks he is exactly the right person. On the other hand, his attentiveness often drives her crazy. She thinks she must also be immature not to like his constant attention.

The conversation goes around and around as the two fourteen-year-olds strain to impart wisdom to each other. They do not feel free to talk to any adult about issues of sex and relationships, and their families never bring up the topic in an information-sharing manner. It is always emotionally loaded. "You don't tell your parents about sex," says Dee. "They just freak out. If you tell them, they think you're a whore or something."

They are so contradictory, says Courtney. "If you tell them that you're not ready to have sex they conclude, 'Oh God, sex is on their mind. They're trying to cover up for it.' They get hysterical. If you tell them that you think you are ready, they're like, 'You're not going out tonight.'"

What her parents couldn't guess and Courtney can't risk telling them is that they are giving her a muddled message. Her concerns hint at a need for boundaries. Courtney, who acts like she hates rules says, "Usually on school nights they won't let me go over to a friend's house, unless they live in the neighborhood, unless we are doing a project." Yet they let her go to Nat's house just to watch television until 10 o'clock on school nights. "They let me go over to my boy-friend's house when they know his parents aren't home. That is weird. I am surprised they let him come over all the time. They're really good about him, they've accepted him, and they always let me hang out with him." It seems just when she wishes there were some limits, her parents have given her an abundance of space.

The Pressure Increases

With all the opportunities she and Nat have to be alone in empty houses, it is getting more difficult for Courtney to draw the line. Nat is increasingly aggressive. "We haven't done anything that's a big deal. He's kissed me. He's gone up my shirt and stuff, but that's all. But you can tell it's going to go farther," she tells Dee.

Courtney, petite and thin, is painfully self-conscious about her whole body, and particularly her stomach. Like too many girls her age she has a distorted body image, imagining she is paunchy. "I have this obsession with stomachs. I'm going to get a flat stomach," Courtney says. "I don't even like to look at myself naked, so why would I expect other people to?" Every time Nat pulls up her shirt, she pulls it down. He asks her why she is so self-conscious. He tells her that her body is beautiful. "I'm like, 'No, no, no.' So he gets frustrated."

One day when Dee and Nat are over, Nat keeps kissing Courtney right in front of Dee. He is all over Courtney, saying he is going to marry her. It is terribly awkward. Finally, in desperation, Courtney uses her period as an excuse. . . .

But the issue keeps coming up. She is relieved when school starts and they can't be together as much. She's still hoping that it "will definitely be okay if I say no, because I don't think I'm ready to have sex in the next few weeks."

Just fifteen, Nat has already had sex with at least three girls. He tells his friends he lost his virginity when he was twelve. Courtney and Dee still think their age, fourteen, is too young. "I don't really think about my age when I think about it. I just think about me," says Courtney. "I think fourteen definitely sounds young, but I think tenth grade is about average. I'm not really excited about it because I don't think many girls enjoy it their first time, and I think it will be painful. But it's something that you want to get over with. I think it's a little too young to come up in relationships, but it is coming up. It's something you have to face. I think you have to deal with it at fourteen, decide."

Time to Deal with It

She has concerns about Nat that never get noticed by her parents. . . .

Courtney found out the reason Nat doesn't like his dad is that he hits him and his mom. She heard from one of her friends that Nat isn't always faithful to his girlfriends. Soon after school began, his behavior became erratic and he ended up being hospitalized again for depression. She doesn't talk to her parents about these things.

Courtney goes back and forth in her mind about Nat. She sometimes has bad feelings about him and is definitely sure she doesn't want to have sex. But she always comes back around. When he was in the mental hospital, she says, she stopped taking him for granted.

She likes him a lot. Maybe she is even infatuated, but she doesn't think she really loves him. "He always used to tell me that he loved me, and he'd always get mad because I wouldn't tell him I loved him," says Courtney. "I only did when he was in the hospital, because I figured, He's in a mental hospital, what else can I do?"

When he is released from the hospital, they continue as before. He'll ask. She'll say, "I don't think so." Then he'll say, "Oh, let's have sex, I want to have sex with you." Then they talk about it.

There is tension. She likes him; she feels she doesn't want to touch so much. That's another thing Nat gets mad about. "He can't wait to touch a girl's body, and then he gets mad at me when I just sit there." Courtney tells him, "I'm sorry. Maybe next time."

For her, making out is enough. "I don't know any girls that are as eager about it as guys," says Courtney. "When girls have sex, they're giving in to guys. Maybe they wanted to, but not as much. I think they just want it because the guy wants it. If they didn't have sex, I don't think they'd be upset. But with guys, I think it upsets them if they don't." Nat is always telling her she has no sex drive. She tells him she's sorry, but that is the way she's always been with all her boyfriends. She's fine with kissing, but she just goes along with anything else. Nat tells her that if a girl with him doesn't "get into it," then he feels like he is forcing himself on her. Courtney doesn't know what to do.

About two and a half months after she starts dating Nat, Courtney runs out of excuses. "I just did it because he really kept bothering me about it." Deep inside she knows part of her hesitation is because she doesn't trust him "not to cheat on me, not to break up with me." But she is worn down. So finally in November when there are two Teacher's Workdays, where students are out of school at the end of the quarter, she does it.

Prelude to Sex

On the Friday before, the two of them are "making out like crazy in the rec room. We had talked about it before and I was like, 'My parents are upstairs. It's not a good idea.' I was trying to stop talking about it." She tells him that maybe when her parents aren't home it would be okay. He jumps at the opportunity.

"I'll come over on Monday," he tells her.

Courtney knows his school has no holiday and immediately tries to persuade him to go. Who's she kidding? He doesn't care at all about school. He insists on coming over Monday. She finally agrees. Now it is planned.

Saturday and Sunday she pushes it out of her mind. "I wasn't really scared. I just didn't think about it."

Then Monday comes and true to his word, Nat arrives at her door. She has the hugest butterflies in her stomach. The worst feelings are about how she is ugly, and now she is going to be naked, and it is going to hurt, but she has to get it out of the way.

They start out sitting on the family room couch watching television. He says, "Let's go upstairs."

She gulps. "Uhhh, why?"

He says, "I don't know, it's better up there."

Courtney wishes her sister would come home, her mother would call, the house would fall down! She whispers, "Fine."

They go upstairs to her bright feminine bedroom complete with pink-and-white mattress-ticking curtains, lace pillows, and crisp white sheets. . . .

Today this familiar haven feels strangely foreign. It is her feminine, teenage preserve and now she is bringing this boy to her bed.

Sex and Humiliation

He undresses. She averts her eyes. She takes off everything but her sweatshirt. She feels so incredibly vulnerable sitting there. "I get really self-conscious. I think that kind of bothers him because he's not self-conscious at all. And that's pretty funny to me because I think the male body is actually pretty ugly."

She keeps on reminding herself that Nat is good to be with because he's been in this situation before. He tries to take off her sweatshirt. She pulls it down over her small breasts. He tells her not to be self-conscious, that he likes her so much and thinks she is perfect. "He was really nice about it," she recalls. "That's good if you're going to have sex with someone to have someone who is ego-boosting about your body." But she never lets him take her shirt off.

She keeps telling herself it is okay, it's not that big a deal. But she has this feeling she is doing it for the wrong reasons.

They lie down and he goes for it vigorously. She never gets involved in the act. It's almost as if it is happening to someone else. It is awkward and clumsy. "He skipped steps," Courtney, more experienced now, remembers. "He'd kiss and then want to have sex. That's not good for me. You've got to work up to it." She tries to let him know she's not ready, but he is oblivious. . . .

The actual sex is a bust. "If a girl's a virgin, it hurts, and it doesn't always work your first try. So we didn't really fully succeed, and I felt dumb. I still don't know if I consider it sex. Technically we had sex," says Courtney, "but it didn't go all the way in."

She senses his disappointment. She feels like a failure. But they don't talk about it at all. There is nothing tender or reassuring. When it is over, he sits up, pulls on his clothes and says, "My mom's picking me up because I have a doctor's appointment. I'll see you later."

Courtney dresses and says, "Okay, 'bye." She feels horrible—embarrassed, unsuccessful, and terribly alone. She doesn't move until she hears the front door close.

The next morning Courtney wakes up feeling totally humiliated. She just wants to forget it ever happened, but she can't stop thinking about it. . . .

Fourteen, Bored, and Unsure

Then Nat breaks up with her. Not right afterwards but several weeks later. Her friends say not to worry about it. . . .

In time Courtney and Nat get back together briefly, but the old magic is gone. "I don't even know whether this is going to be a good relationship, if we're going to go out for another three months or whether it will only be a few weeks," says Courtney. Before, Nat used to tell her he loved her all the time. Now he never says it and she wishes he did. But she never tells him how she feels.

Nat and Courtney break up for good the day before Valentine's Day. He had been cheating on her even while they continued to have sex. Still fifteen, Nat is now on his fifth or sixth sexual partner.

Courtney is sad. "I kind of miss having a boyfriend, but not Nat himself. I miss someone in the role of a boyfriend—going out at night, talking to him on the phone, going to his house. I used to hang out with my friends and my boyfriend. I have my friends but where is my boyfriend?"

Only fourteen, Courtney has had sex, has carried on a full-blown social life in the middle of the night, smoked cigarettes and pot, cut classes, been with somebody who "stole" his parents' car and somebody who has been hospitalized for psychiatric problems. By her freshman year, she was bored with legitimate school activities.

As for sex, she thinks that maybe when she is older, "like in college or after college, I'll have a steady boyfriend, and then sex would be like a bigger part of my life. But now that I've had this bad experience, I'm not sure anymore."

CHAPTER 2

SEXUAL ORIENTATION: GAY AND LESBIAN TEENS

Contemporary Issues
Companion

THE REALITIES OF GROWING UP GAY

Richard Jerome

Gay adolescents often face hostility from others and suffer all kinds of indignities because of their sexuality. According to the following article from *People Weekly* magazine by Richard Jerome, although the immediate families of young gays and lesbians tend to be more accepting today than in past years, the same is not always true of their peers. School is torture for many gay and lesbian teens who experience verbal harassment every day, as well as beatings and other physical harassment. Such overt hostility causes many homosexual teenagers to feel fear, self-shame, and emotional confusion, leading them to turn to drugs or to resort to suicide. On the other hand, the article reports, some gay and lesbian teens choose to fight back, determined to make society accept them on their own terms.

Compact, with faintly Cagneyesque features, Jamie Nabozny has the look of a Dead End Kid and the soul of a social worker—which is what he wants to be someday. Certainly he has some familiarity with the field. At age 11, depressed and withdrawn, he ran away from home in little Ashland, Wis. He was quickly retrieved but tried to kill himself that same year, swallowing a handful of his mother's Midol and prescription painkillers. By ninth grade, Nabozny had made two more suicide attempts and had spent three stretches in psychiatric wards.

Compounding his anguish was the abuse he endured at the hands of his schoolmates—taunts, shoves, beatings and, in his freshman year in high school, a galling humiliation. One morning when he went to the bathroom, he was accosted by two boys. "One pushed his knees into the back of mine," says Nabozny, now 22. "I fell into the urinal, and another kid started peeing on me. I just remember sitting there, waiting for it to get over with."

Nabozny's shame, confusion and relentless persecution all grew out of one simple fact: He is gay.

Facing Facts

Even in the best of circumstances, adolescence is a purgatory of hormonal and emotional turbulence. But for teenagers who are homosexual—and various estimates place their number at from 5 to 10 percent of U.S. high school students—it is a time of fear, shame and potentially devastating emotional hazards. According to the most comprehensive poll of randomly chosen youths—a 1995 survey of more than 4,000 students conducted by the Massachusetts Department of Education—the high school years are rife with abuse of homosexuals, some of it self-inflicted. Gay males and lesbians were five times more likely than straight kids to skip school out of fear for their safety and almost five times more likely to use cocaine. Even more alarming: According to the survey, a stunning 36.5 percent of gay and lesbian high schoolers try to kill themselves each year—this in an era when the openly gay Rupert Everett is a rising movie star and Elton John practically defines middle-of-the-road pop culture.

"People ask, 'Well, isn't it better today than it was a generation ago? Ellen [DeGeneres] is out on TV and so on,'" says Rea Carey, executive director of the National Youth Advocacy Coalition in Washington, D.C., a nonprofit clearinghouse for gay issues. "Some things are better, but there's a tremendous backlash. As young people take courageous steps in coming out, they get slammed against a wall for doing it."

Indeed, many Americans continue to view homosexuality as a character defect to be controlled or reformed. In June 1998, for instance, Senate Majority Leader Trent Lott likened gays and lesbians to "sinners, addicts and kleptomaniacs." But the weight of research indicates that people don't select their sexuality. "The evidence we now have strongly suggests that this is determined," says University of Massachusetts (Amherst) professor of neuroscience Geert J. De Vries. "It's not purely genetic, but there doesn't seem to any choice in the matter. One thing that is clear is that the brains of homosexuals and heterosexuals appear to be different. Studies suggest that homosexuals in many cases developed neurologically in a way that made them more likely to become homosexual."

The issue of sexual orientation generally lies buried until kids enter puberty, when they find it increasingly difficult to ignore impulses that may seem strange and unwelcome. "I kind of started getting a feeling when I was in sixth grade—like walking down the hall I was supposed to be looking at Sue, and instead I was looking at John or Bob," says Nathan Postell IV, now 21, of Raleigh, N.C. "By the time I was 14, I knew I was different. There was no question about it. I had crushes on my teachers—I just thought, you know, how attractive or masculine Mr. So-and-So was. I was like, okay, I'm gay, so now what do I do? One day I was watching Divorce Court, and this guy was leaving his wife for another man. He was swishing around and doing this whole thing, so I was kind of practicing how to swish. I just thought that was how you were supposed to do it."

Sixth grade was also a pivotal year for Kelli Peterson of Salt Lake City. "I had a crush on my [female] friend instead of the boy all the other girls liked," she says. "In the beginning I didn't even have a word for what I was feeling. But then when I was about 13, I started hearing kids call other kids 'fag,' and I learned what it meant." More than anything, she was terrified. "I thought all homosexuals were men and that they all had AIDS and were child molesters and lived in San Francisco," says Peterson, now 20. "I also thought all of them were going to hell. I started going to church and praying not to be gay." Working at it, she plastered her walls with pictures of actor Luke Perry and other heartthrobs. "Boys, boys, boys," she told herself, "I've got to think about nothing except boys." She even started dating them, but when kissing time arrived, she says, "I'd just turn my brain off. I couldn't bring myself to get close to them."

In hindsight, at least, Jamie Nabozny recalls feeling the first stirrings of homosexuality long before puberty. "I was like 6 or 7," he says. "I was in school, and we played house. Everybody played house. It was the normal thing. But I knew I wanted to be married to a man. I said, 'Why can't I be a guy and marry a guy?' I think the teacher looked down on it—like, 'Well, that's not how things are supposed to be.'"

Facing Family

It was the beginning of his downward spiral. "Once I realized I was different—and that other people realized—I became very introverted," he says. Instead of socializing after school, Nabozny remained cloistered in his room: "I was afraid that if I participated, people would know more about me. That scared me."

Most daunting of all was the prospect of discussing his sexuality with his family. Nabozny's first impulse was to avoid the issue: One day when he was 11, he ran away to a friend's home, a couple of miles from his family's. He was brought home by a sympathetic juvenile officer who, after hearing Jamie's story, lifted his burden and told Carol and Robert Nabozny their son was gay. "My parents started crying—they said they loved me and it didn't matter," Nabozny recalls. "But my dad said, 'I think he'll change. I think it's a phase.'" Robert Nabozny concedes he was caught off guard. "It struck me hard," he admits. "My first thought was 'Not my son—ain't no way.'" But Carol wasn't surprised: "Being his mother, I knew something was different about him."

For many young gays, gaining acceptance from their immediate families has gotten easier than it might have been a few years ago, though the moment of reckoning remains fraught with enormous anxiety. "How could I tell my parents I was gay?" says Kelli Peterson. "I didn't even dare to admit it to myself." But Randy Peterson and his wife, Dee, both 45, were actually relieved when, at 17, Kelli sat in a cafe and tearfully poured out her heart. Like Nabozny, Kelli had weathered taunts, schoolyard fights and despondency, and in March 1994 she had overdosed on painkillers, leading to a brief stay in a psychiatric clinic. "Suddenly I knew why she'd been so depressed, and my heart just ached for her," says Dee, a mailroom supervisor at the University of Utah Hospital. "I was more upset when Kelli told me she was a socialist," adds Randy, a copy editor at *The Salt Lake Tribune* who now believes that gay adolescents should come out sooner rather than later. "Pull the Band-Aid off all at once," he says, "instead of a little at a time."

Nathan Postell experienced the relief of full disclosure at 16—with a little help from the cable guy. "He had to rewire my room and my mom had to move my bed," explains Postell, whose family was living in Brandywine, Md., at the time. "She found certain reading material." A short time later, Sandra Gibson questioned her son while driving her car. "I said, 'I'm gay—I like other men,'" he remembers. "I was sick to my stomach. I was nervous. I was shaking and I kept saying, like, 'Oh, my God' over and over." But his mother proved broadminded. "Her main question was, 'So I'm never going to have grandkids?' By the time we got home, she said, 'Nathan, it's going to be okay. I still love you.'" Says Gibson simply: "He was still Nathan."

Targets of Abuse

Yet the world outside the home is often less tolerant. Sometimes insult turns into assault.

At 16, Willi Wagner didn't blend easily into the crowd on the streets of Fayetteville, Ark. Six feet tall, with shoulder-length hair and two-inch nails (often polished in glittery colors), he was fond of dressing in eccentric garb—including long robes. "I just loved the whole Egyptian thing and that angular look," says Wagner (who at 17 now favors a clean-cut style). He has been open about his gayness since ninth grade and has no regrets. "The better you know who you are, the better you're going to be with other people," he says.

Still, he paid for his candor. Mostly the harassment was verbal, and Wagner gave as good as he got. "They'd call me a faggot and I'd call them a hick," Wagner says. "One time a guy wrote 'Willi is a fagot' on the blackboard. I just loved that he couldn't even spell it—I never let him forget that." But things turned ugly, as police photos attest, on Dec. 2, 1996. At about 11:30 A.M., Willi and some friends were walking to Fayetteville's Hog Wash Laundry (a coin laundry that serves hot dogs) when eight teenage boys piled out of a car and a blue pickup. After one hollered "Come here, you f—king faggot," five of them formed a circle around Wagner while the others attacked him. "One of the kids was kicking him in the back with cowboy boots," says Fayetteville Police Det. John Gentry. "That's pretty bad." Wagner was left with a black eye, bruised kidneys and his nose broken in two places. "I could feel my nose crack," he says. "It was not a good feeling."

Two juveniles were sentenced to probation for the assault, which was covered widely by local media. ("I'm the local famous fag," says

Willi sarcastically.) Wagner and his parents, Bill, 44, a Wal-Mart optician's assistant, and Carolyn, a homemaker, who turns 45 on Aug. 15, 1998, have received abusive phone calls and had anti-gay screeds stuffed in their mailbox. Enraged, Carolyn pressed area merchants to post "Hate-Free Zone" signs. "I have to work every day," she says, "at not hating the haters."

The travails of kids like Willi Wagner and statistics on gay adolescent suicide moved some Dallas educators to open Walt Whitman Community School, "the only private school in the nation for gay teens," says director Becky Thompson, 47. After a year her enrollment numbered 15 students, and in fall 1998 she expects it will rise to 20 or 25. "Right now," Thompson says, "we're on a hope and a dream."

From Acceptance to Activism

Despite all the obstacles, it is still possible to grow up gay, healthy and safe within the educational mainstream. At 20, Jeremy Ferguson, a native of Everett, Wash., north of Seattle, appears fully at ease with his homosexuality. "My school had a respect policy," he says. "There was zero tolerance for harassment." Ferguson thrived in that climate, editing the school paper and getting himself elected a student parliamentarian. He was secure enough to bring a male date to the senior prom—they wore matching tuxedos—and for a year or so Jeremy sold ads for the *Seattle Gay News*. (He now works for a San Francisco pharmaceutical company.) He also spoke on behalf of Hands Off Washington, a group that worked unsuccessfully to pass a gay rights bill in Washington state. "I knew Jeremy was going to do something big with his life," Julie Ferguson, 42, says of her son. "I just didn't picture he'd be a gay activist."

In fact, an increasing number of young gays have become activists, on the theory that society may not fully accept them unless it is pushed. Kelli Peterson—who once begged God for deliverance from her homosexuality—might seem an unlikely firebrand. But after coming out to her parents and peers ("I'm a lesbian!" she blurted to her startled drama class one day, exasperated by years of innuendo), Kelli grew more at ease with herself. Soon, Peterson and about 20 other students formed a gay-straight alliance, which they hoped to have formally recognized by their school. "When Kelli tried to start the club, I started calling her 'Kelli Rosa,' as in Rosa Parks," says Barbara Murdock, then her creative-writing teacher. "She refused to sit at the back of the bus."

The Salt Lake City School Board was not enthusiastic: Rather than recognize Peterson's group, it voted 4 to 3 to ban all extracurricular clubs—the only way it could ban the club without running afoul of federal civil-rights statutes. "I took the board's decision as a declaration of war," Peterson says. "It made me an activist."

Now studying psychology at Salt Lake City Community College—

and dating schoolmate Mary Callis, 17—Peterson speaks frequently at gay-rights rallies. She succeeded Greg Louganis as spokesperson for the Gay/Lesbian Straight Teachers Network and in 1997 won a $5,000 Playboy Foundation Hugh Hefner First Amendment Person of Conscience Award. ("No," she says, "you won't be seeing me as a centerfold.")

But no American adolescent has had more of an impact on the plight of his gay peers than Jamie Nabozny. After a beating in his junior year forced him to undergo exploratory abdominal surgery, he left Ashland High for good. Time and again, he and his parents had complained to school officials about the relentless harassment, but nothing was done to protect him. Finally Nabozny sued the Ashland school district. The case was thrown out, but in July 1996 he won a landmark victory in a federal appellate court in Chicago, which held that schools and school officials could be sued for failing to address anti-gay abuse. "That blows my mind—it was the first time the government ever acknowledged gay teens," says Nabozny. He pursued his action in federal court, which found the administrators guilty of discrimination but did not hold the school district liable. Nabozny settled for $900,000 and now tours the country speaking on gay issues. "This one kid in Texas came up to me and said, 'When I was in high school, I had the biggest picture of you on my locker. Every day the thing that got me through all of my classes was knowing you were going to be there.'" Jamie Nabozny knew how important that was, because nobody but his family had been there for him.

Gay and Lesbian Relationships: Going Steady

Jon Barrett

Jon Barrett is an editor with the *Advocate,* a national gay and lesbian magazine. In the following article, Barrett writes that gay and lesbian teens are coming out at an earlier age and are much more open about their dating lives than their peers were in the recent past. He reports that this new openness can be attributed primarily to the Internet and to the hundreds of gay student groups that now exist, both of which provide these teens with more opportunities to meet and support each other. In Barrett's view, gay and lesbian youths today are able to do something they could not have done several years ago—to learn the same lessons of growing up through their romantic relationships that straight teens have always been able to experience openly.

Marc Robinson, a 17-year-old from Milwaukee, didn't know how good he had it until the day he spoke to a group of gay senior citizens. "It was weird to hear how they weren't able to come out until they were, like, 50," he says. "They didn't know what it was like to be with someone. Then, when they [did finally date], they had the same type of problems teenagers have with their first relationships."

Although the stories the seniors told Robinson may have had an "I walked 10 miles in three feet of snow" quality, they vividly illustrate how times have changed. That's especially true when the seniors' experiences are compared with Robinson's: Out of the closet at 15, he's had three relationships, the longest lasting five months. "I know people who have been in relationships for, like, two years," he says. "I have two lesbian friends who are never apart. Like, if you say one of their names, you say the other. That's just how it is."

A New Openness

And that's just how it is for thousands of high school students across the country. Despite the very real threats of verbal and physical abuse many of them still face, gay teens are not only coming out younger every year, they're also leading openly gay dating lives with a panache

Reprinted from "Going Steady," by Jon Barrett, *The Advocate*, April 10, 2001. Used with permission of Liberation Publications, Inc.

that would surprise gay people only 10 years their senior.

Take 18-year-old Peter Viengkham and 18-year-old David Purtz, for example. The suburban Fort Lauderdale, Fla., couple have dated off and on for more than a year. They even occasionally spend nights together in their parents' homes. "My mom knows we're going to have sex anyhow," Viengkham says. "She's like, 'I don't want them to do it in a car because we won't allow them to do it here.'"

Or consider 17-year-old June Washington and 18-year-old Jeanette Sanders of Philadelphia. The two have been going steady ever since their first date a year and a half ago, when they went to see the film *Double Jeopardy*. "It turned out we didn't see much of the movie," Sanders says, acknowledging, almost under her breath, that she and Washington shared their first kiss in the back row of the theater that night.

"These kids are coming out and experiencing things that I should have at their age," says 32-year-old Javier Smith, who leads a gay youth group in Boise, Idaho. "A lot of times they surprise me with their maturity and the things that they've done. But other times I'm surprised at how immature they are, and I have to remind myself that they are only 16 or 17."

Aside from the Internet, gay student groups—there are more than 800 of them registered with the Gay, Lesbian, and Straight Education Network—are the biggest reason for the upsurge in out and proud dating among teens, says Caitlin Ryan, coauthor of *Lesbian & Gay Youth: Care and Counseling*. "It was difficult 10 years ago for a gay youth to meet another gay youth," Ryan says. "But these groups are providing an opportunity to have peers and to learn about being gay through your peers."

Gay Student Groups Bring Teens Together

According to a survey conducted by Lisa Love, a health education specialist whose work includes gay youth issues in the Seattle school district, the two topics, besides coming out, that members of these groups want to talk about most are dating and sex. "Kids are either talking about relationships they're in, they've been in, or frustrated that they're not in," Love says. Even though many of the groups do not directly address dating issues, they bring teens together in an atmosphere in which they can at last enjoy the same rites of passage that their straight peers take for granted.

In Boise, for example, the youth group is the primary social outlet for gay teens, including 17-year-old Nick Rutley and 18-year-old Kayla Tabb. The only openly gay student at his high school, Rutley says he "would be beaten alive" if he were seen holding hands or kissing Travis Harrison, the 16-year-old he's been dating for the past few weeks. Nevertheless, he and Harrison plan to go to the prom together. "I'm a little bit nervous," Rutley says. "I've talked to my parents, I've talked to the principal, and I've talked to a lot of my friends and asked them to be there, just for safety in numbers."

Tabb started dating when she was 16 and has had two girlfriends, both of whom were 20 years old. However, she's not currently dating. "I've got too much stuff going on right now just with trying to finish high school," she says. She did recently try to date the one other girl who regularly attends the youth group, but "it was supposed to be sort of a messing-around sort of thing, and she wanted a relationship," Tabb says. "So I decided it needed to stop."

Viengkham helped establish the gay student group at his high school but met Purtz on America Online. "Everybody I know happens to meet people on AOL," he says. "I met other people [online] before David, but I guess you would call those flings," Viengkham says. "David was the first person I went out with, technically. Once we met, he actually drove up to my house. It was a really fast kind of thing, like, 'Oh, let's meet.'"

Parents' Reactions

While just meeting someone used to be the biggest dating-related obstacle for gay teens, today's youth say their dating conundrums aren't so different from the ones their straight peers face, including how to tell parents about relationships.

Washington and Sanders haven't come out to their parents about their sexual orientation or about the year and a half they've been dating. "To talk to [my mom] would be tough," Sanders says. "I mean, she sort of knows stuff and asks about it, but I never verify." The couple only came out to their friends when they realized they needed the support they weren't finding at home. "We decided we needed to tell people [about the relationship] because whenever we got into problems with each other, there was nobody to turn to," Sanders says.

Those, like Viengkham, who can talk to their parents often turn to them when the relationship gets bumpy. "My mom gives me advice and says, 'Maybe he doesn't know you're feeling that way,' or 'Maybe you should talk to him,'" Viengkham says. Others, like Tabb, say their parents try almost too hard to be accepting. "My mom will bring things home and say, 'Look, this has a rainbow on it,'" Tabb says. Still, she says, it was comforting to tell her mother about her first girlfriend: "She gave me a big hug, and then she started to cry."

Where sex fits into the relationship—if at all—is another cause for concern, especially for a generation hit with images from TV shows like *Queer as Folk*, which often equates gay life with no-strings sexual encounters. But many teens seem to take a more cautious approach than the boys on Showtime. "I'm going to wait for quite some time before I even consider having sex with [Harrison]," Rutley says. "I have to know that [our relationship] isn't just casual, that there is a commitment of sorts."

Viengkham says his gay friends are more sexually active than his lesbian friends, but he doubts the difference is as much a gay-versus-lesbian thing as a male-versus-female thing. "I could go up to any straight guy or any gay guy and ask them how much sex goes through their mind, and they would answer honestly, 'All the time,'" he says.

Breaking Up Is Hard

The hardest part of all, of course, is when a relationship ends. "Initiating relationships, especially in a small town like this, is often nothing more than 'I'm gay and you're gay,'" says Boise youth-group leader Smith. "But I sometimes spend night after night answering phone calls at 10 o'clock at night from kids asking me the same question over and over again: 'Why did they break up with me?'"

Indeed, breakups are one point where gay teens diverge from their straight friends. The end of a relationship can underscore just how little gay relationships are recognized.

"Gay youth want to be in relationships for the same reasons other youth do," Ryan says. "And I think it's wonderful that there are so many opportunities for them to find each other so they can actually date in high school. But when they break up and the nature of the relationship isn't really understood by their peers or their family, I think that can be an extremely isolating and vulnerable time."

However, feelings of isolation and vulnerability are exactly what teens are supposed to be experiencing at this age. Relationships are about personal growth and experience—and sometimes the pain that goes with them. Now more than ever, gay and lesbian youths are able to learn the lessons of growing up at the same time their straight peers do. "I learned a lot in my last relationship, and I've learned a lot being single," says Harrison. "I've definitely had a lot less emotional pain being single than being in a relationship. In the end, what motivates me to be involved in another serious relationship again is [simply] the desire to love and be loved."

THE INTERNET: A REFUGE FOR GAY AND LESBIAN TEENS

Jennifer Egan

In the following selection, Jennifer Egan focuses on the impact that the Internet has had on gay and lesbian teens in recent years. The Internet helps young gay and lesbian teens to feel less isolated, she explains, by giving them a place where they can acknowledge their sexual identity and form relationships with others who accept them as they are. Through Internet romances, she notes, many gay and lesbian teens can experience the same age-appropriate emotions and personal development as their straight peers. The accessibility of information about homosexuality on the Internet has also played an important role in lowering the age at which young people first identify themselves as gay, Egan writes. However, she cautions, there are several dangers associated with the gay online community, such as older men who conceal their true identity to prey on teens. Egan is a novelist and a frequent contributor to the *New York Times Magazine*.

In the summer of 1999, when he was 15, a youth I will refer to by only his first name, Jeffrey, finally admitted to himself that he was gay. This discovery had been coming on for some time; he had noticed that he felt no attraction to girls and that he became aroused when showering with other boys after physical education class. But Jeffrey is a devout Southern Baptist, attending church several times each week, where, he says, the pastor seems to make a point of condemning homosexuality. Jeffrey knew of no homosexuals in his high school or in his small town in the heart of the South. (He asked that I withhold not only his last name but also any other aspects of his life that might reveal his identity.) He prayed that his errant feelings were a phase. But as the truth gradually settled over him, he told me in the summer of 2000 during a phone conversation punctuated by nervous visits to his bedroom door to make sure no family member was listening in, he became suicidal.

"I'm a Christian—I'm like, how could God possibly do this to me?" he said. "My mother's always saying, 'It'll be so wonderful when you

47

meet that beautiful Christian girl and have lots of grandchildren,' and every time she said that, I was like, That's it: my life is going to be hell."

He called a crisis line for gay teenagers, where a counselor suggested he attend a gay support group in a city an hour and a half away. But being 15, he was too young to drive and afraid to enlist his parents' help in what would surely seem a bizarre and suspicious errand. It was around this time that Jeffrey first typed the words "gay" and "teen" into a search engine on the computer he'd gotten several months before and was staggered to find himself aswirl in a teeming online gay world, replete with resource centers, articles, advice columns, personals, chat rooms, message boards, porn sites and—most crucially—thousands of closeted and anxious kids like himself. That discovery changed his life.

"The Internet is the thing that has kept me sane," he told me. "I live constantly in fear. I can't be my true self. My mom complains: 'I can see you becoming more detached from us. You're always spending time on the computer.' But the Internet is my refuge."

Creating an Online Persona

Jeffrey and I met when he responded to an online message I posted, seeking gay teenagers willing to discuss their online lives. When we were first getting to know each other, he made it clear that he could allow no overlap between his online gay life and the life he led in the "real world." He explained, "In our town, everybody knows everybody, and everybody knows everybody's business." He feared that if word of his sexual orientation were to reach his parents, they might refuse to support him or pay for college. From his peers at school he dreaded violence, and with good reason: according to a 1996 study of the Seattle public schools, one in six gay teenagers is beaten so badly during adolescence that he requires medical attention.

Jeffrey's computer is in his bedroom, garrisoned inside a thicket of codes and passwords. While he uses the Internet to communicate with high-school friends—Jeffrey is now 16 and a junior in high school—and to pursue his avid fandom of the group 'N Sync, he has separate screen names and "instant messaging" services for these activities. (An instant message, or I.M., allows two or more people to engage in a real-time dialogue on screen.) This way, no one from his "straight life" can track his forays into the online gay world using the "locate" feature on America Online, for example, which allows subscribers to find online "buddies" in whatever public chat room or other AOL area they happen to be visiting—a potential disaster for gay teenagers. A brainy, ebullient kid, Jeffrey is an excellent student, active in high-school government, with a number of close friends. He took a girl as his date to homecoming. But his free time belongs largely to the disembodied gay life he pursues online—from 8:30 P.M. to 2 A.M. during the school year, and for even longer stretches in summertime.

Jeffrey was hesitant to explore the online gay world at first, he said, certain he would somehow get caught. "I thought, Somebody's gonna get in my computer and find out," he said. "The paranoia was that bad." So he did the obvious thing—the thing many Web pundits advise as a matter of safety when communicating with strangers online: he employed an alias, changed the town he came from and then threw in a few other "improvements" on his real identity. He said he came from a rich family, drove a BMW, had killer good looks and was 18—old enough to cruise the adult gay chat rooms.

But as his online friendships deepened, the phony elements of Jeffrey's story began to oppress him: "I was like, I can't be myself in real life, and I come on the Internet and I still can't be myself. Yeah, I'm gay, but it's a lie." In June 2000, he mustered his nerve and began telling his online friends that he was not quite the person they had believed. "One of my really good gay friends has nothing to do with me now," he told me sadly one month after "coming out" online as his real self. . . .

By the summer of 2000, Jeffrey also had an online boyfriend, whom I will call C., the first initial of his first name. A fellow Southerner a year older than Jeffrey whom Jeffrey called his "true love," though the two had never met, C. forgave him his online fabrications but pointed out that they complicated things. "After I told C.," Jeffrey explained, "he said, 'I still love you, but I don't know you.'"

A Heightened Awareness of Sexual Orientation

For homosexual teenagers with computer access, the Internet has, quite simply, revolutionized the experience of growing up gay. Isolation and shame persist among gay teenagers, of course, but now, along with the inhospitable families and towns in which many find themselves marooned, there exists a parallel online community—real people like them in cyberspace with whom they can chat, exchange messages and even engage in (online) sex. The popularity of "cybering," as online sex is called—masturbating in real time to sexually explicit typed messages—has lately been supplemented (among boys, especially) with a mania for Web cams and microphones, which allow them to see and hear each other masturbate, using programs like Microsoft's NetMeeting. But this is only as important for gay boys as it no doubt is for the countless straight youths who flock to Internet sex sites. What was most critical to the gay kids I spoke with was the simple, revelatory discovery that they were not alone.

Indeed, gay teenagers surfing the Net can find Web sites packed with information about homosexuality and about local gay support groups and counseling services, along with coming-out testimonials from young people around the world. Gay pornography, too, can be a valuable resource; a number of youths I spoke with, male and female, said that the availability of online porn had proved critical to their discovery of their sexual orientation. Kyle, a 15-year-old youth from Florida I met online, wrote me in an e-mail message: "What I did was go into gay chat sites on AOL and ask where I could find free gay porno sites, my first gay porn I had ever seen. The pictures turned me on soooo much, and I loved it. It was just so clear to me, I am gay and I like men." I asked him how old he was when this happened. "I was about 11," he replied.

Parents' attempts to restrict their children's access to hard-core Web sites are rarely a match for their kids' surpassing computer skills. (Several teenagers I spoke with said they had accessed gay pornography on computers at school.) Which means that a curious teenager not only has ready access to graphic material, but also can engage in sexual experimentation with peers that would be next to impossible in everyday life. As one 13-year-old put it in an e-mail message, "I could say that the Internet made my life a living hell. . . . It made me realize I'm different. I hated it . . . but then I realized the Net helped me realize I'm gay. . . . I'd rather find out now than when I'm 30 and married to my wife with two kids or something."

Recent studies suggest that kids are identifying themselves as gay at much younger ages; among males the average age has dropped from 19–21 to 14–16, and in females from their early 20's to 15–16. Caitlin Ryan, a clinical social worker and the author of *Lesbian and Gay Youth: Care and Counseling,* says, "Today, youths are coming out right in the middle of high school or earlier, and I think the Internet is playing an important role in that because it's providing information to help them label those feelings and figure out who they really are."

One might reasonably ask whether such heightened early awareness of sexual orientation is always a good thing. And for all the educational resources the cyberworld can offer gay youth—articles and studies and hot-line numbers and so on—the gay-sex cyberworld, like the much larger straight-sex one, is not an especially wholesome environment in which to tease apart one's sexuality. Type the words "gay" and "teen" into virtually any search engine, and you'll find yourself circling among interlocking porn sites, some featuring "twinks," or boys of allegedly legal age who appear to be younger (and in some cases obviously are), and other sites hawking lesbian scenes that clearly cater to heterosexual men. And of course, there is the simple fact that cyberspace is an incorporeal world, a world without flesh-and-blood people, and thus a peculiar realm in which to become one's "true self," as Jeffrey put it.

"The Internet is an inferior substitute for real-live human beings," says Kevin Jennings, executive director of the Gay, Lesbian and Straight Education Network, a national organization working to end antigay bias in schools. "But it's frankly better than nothing, which is what gay youth have had before.". . .

An Online Girlfriend

Like Jeffrey, many of the boys I talked to described themselves as "addicted" to the Internet. Girls, who responded in smaller numbers to my postings, seemed more aware of the Internet's limitations. They were also more likely to have at least one off-line confidante—a parent, a friend, even several friends—who knew about their sexual orientation and accepted it. In the case of Jane, a 13-year-old African-American girl I met online, her mother knows, but with one exception her friends don't, and she's quite lonely in her eighth-grade class.

"The only word I can think of to describe it is small," she wrote in an e-mail message in the summer of 2000. "People seem to be pretty narrow-minded. . . . It's hard finding a niche anywhere. Even so I mostly hang around with the popular crowd. . . . I'm not trendy. I mean I don't wear sweater sets. LOL."

Online, Jane, who says she has known she was gay since the fifth grade, has been able to find a number of lesbian girls her own age. "I have at least five people on my buddy list that are 13," she said. "The longest going thing I have is with my girlfriend. We've known each other online for 9 or 10 months." Like Jeffrey and C., Jane and her girlfriend, who lives four hours away, had not met. "In ways it's the same as a face-to-face relationship," Jane explained in one e-mail message, adding, "The only difference being that we don't see each other."

When I asked Jane whether having an online girlfriend—whom I will call S.—would keep her from pursuing a relationship with someone she met in person, she wrote, "I would probably be at a crossroad because S. means so much to me. Ya never know tho."

A week later, Jane mentioned in an instant message that she and S. had broken up. . . .

Two months later, as school began, Jane wrote to me: "S. e-mailed me earlier today saying she didn't think she was gay and that it was probably just a phase. Where does the drama end?"

The drama doesn't end, of course; these are *teenagers*. The remarkable thing is that via the Internet, gay teenagers are now able to partake of the normal Sturm und Drang of adolescent life, which before was largely off limits to them. "Now that we have youth who are coming out during adolescence, that means they can experience the normal developmental milestones in time as opposed to off-time," says Caitlin Ryan. "If you have to delay being an adolescent until later in life, I don't think it's a healthy thing."

Jeffrey told me once, speaking of his relationship with C.: "I think it's almost like an accelerated relationship. You can't go out to the movies, so there's nothing to fill the space. You have to talk. It creates this intimacy between you; it draws you closer. Our relationship isn't based on looks or financial status or anything physical. There's no space fillers, because you can't just sit there for 15 minutes and not say anything."

And while language itself seems to buckle against the vagaries of online experience—phrases like "I met. . . ." and "I talked to. . . ." are too easily confused with RL (real life)—there is something of the schoolyard and the mall in the hours of hanging out that many teenagers, gay and straight, do on their computers each night. To understand the texture of this online loitering, I got in the habit of asking gay teenagers what they had on their screens at a particular moment—it was usually some combination of homework, e-mail, games, browser searches, chat rooms and, most of all, instant-messaging sessions—often several at one time. . . .

The Threat from Older Men

The prospect of older men preying on teenagers is a very real issue in the online gay community—though the problem is by no means limited to gays. Jeff Edelman, president of the Student Center, a Web community for college students and high-school students, straight and gay, says that he worries equally about the danger of older men preying on young girls in the heterosexual chat rooms. And in lesbian teenage chat rooms, there is a recurrent suspicion that fellow "teenagers" might actually be straight men seeking out lesbian fantasies.

Among gay teenage boys, the attitude toward older men (known as oldies or sugar daddies) ranges from amusement to weary frustration over the fact that, rather than serving as friends and guides, the men seem to care only for sex. One boy I spoke with told me about an older man who'd tracked him down in his hometown after a conversation on the Internet. The boy eventually filed a restraining order against the man and still worries that he will be stalked again.

But most of the run-ins I heard of between teenage boys and older men were less aggressive than that and ranged in tone from consensual to creepy. Kyle, the 15-year-old from Florida, told me about an online relationship of several weeks he had with a fellow 15-year-old who later admitted he was actually 30 and married, with three children of his own. "He even had a picture of himself," Kyle marveled in an e-mail message. "Come to find out, that picture was his godson, really sick! He seemed to know everything about teen life, like he knew what clothes were popular, and how we talked, stupid abbreviations like Phat for cool. . . . He seemed so real, I would have never guessed."

Ultimately, the man confessed. "He told me he had been lying to me about a FEW things," Kyle wrote. "When I read that, my stomach about dropped to my knees. I flipped. Here I was trusting him with every word I typed, and he LIED about everything. It was a huge shock.". . .

A Need to Be Careful

After recovering from the shock of the 30-year-old's posing as a teen, Kyle began an online relationship in the summer of 2000 with a 16-year-old named Brad, whom he described to me as "the sweetest, nicest guy I had ever met online." He went on to write: "It's weird, we were talking the other day about what we thought was really hot. We both agreed that we thought sitting home and hanging out watching TV or playing board games was a really big turn on."

Kyle and Brad moved from instant messaging to the telephone, and Brad, who lives 10 miles away, was pushing for a face-to-face meeting. Kyle was reluctant. "I can't figure out why I don't want to meet him," he wrote to me. "Maybe I am so afraid of him not liking me. It would be my first physical relationship."

In fact, there are excellent reasons for Kyle's reluctance, and Web sites geared toward gay youth abound with precautions for those who insist on meeting face to face with people they know only through the Net: be sure to meet in a public place; take a friend along or make sure someone knows where you're going; never get in anyone's car. Nonetheless, a majority of gay teenagers I spoke with had met at least one person they had gotten to know over the Internet. (Among lesbian teenagers, real-world meetings seem to be less common.) Some had formed permanent relationships; others had hooked up with older men and had sex—sometimes safe sex, other times not.

A young man I corresponded with who advises gay teenagers through the Gay Student Center Web site recommends viewing multiple pictures of a person before actually meeting, and ideally, speaking to them via Web cam to make sure that picture and person match up. "This I learned the hard way," he wrote in an e-mail message. "I was about 17 and decided I wanted to meet this 'kid' that I met online. I went to the local coffee shop to see my 17-year-old 5-9 blue-eyed stud turn into a 49-year-old, 300-pound dud. . . . He definitely passed himself off as a teen online, he was into the teen scene and was up-to-date. I walked out without speaking to him."

Of course, there is no way to make sure that the picture you've been sent is of the person you've been talking to; pictures of cute teenagers are floating all over the Net, and even some teenagers themselves admit that they've co-opted pictures of total strangers and pretended to be those people for online sexual encounters. According to the Gay Student Center adviser I exchanged e-mail with, plenty of pictures are simply fake. "If the picture looks too good to be true, then it probably is," he said, "especially if they only have one picture and it's really high quality." He also urges teenagers to pay attention to typing and spelling skills; "oldies" (whom he defines as over 40) are usually better typists and spellers than teens. . . .

The Paradox of the Internet

Vanishing friends and intimates are frequent laments among gay teenagers; L.B., a 13-year-old from a Middle Atlantic state, had an online relationship with a 15-year-old boy who he says provided him with enormous guidance and support. L.B. had called the boy at home several times, and had even spoken with two of his siblings. Then, suddenly, the older boy's e-mail address stopped working. When L.B. called his house, the number had been disconnected. "I tried to look for him in directories and stuff," L.B. said. "Couldn't find him so I gave up."

During an e-mail exchange with Fred, an 18-year-old student at a community college who is still closeted, I felt as if I were hearing the other half of the very same anecdote.

"I've had several online relationships over the past few months, and I'm not proud to admit that I broke them off rather shoddily," Fred wrote. "It would go like this: I would set up an obscure e-mail name that I thought would have little connection to anything about me. I meet a guy online, we start to talk, and get to know each other better. Then I become afraid (I don't know what of and I don't know why) and simply stop talking to him. I don't even check the e-mail address I had set up for this guy. I would then stop all gay activity on the Internet for about 3–4 weeks, then I would get a new e-mail address, and I'd do it all over again."

In an instant message, he added: "It's kinda depressing to open up an old account and read those e-mails. . . . They're all like 'Where are you?' 'Why aren't you talking to me?' I feel really bad about it now, especially one guy who lived close to me, and wanted to meet me. . . . I was afraid he was straight and was looking for some fag to beat up."

A paradox emerges from these conversations: while the Internet provides a safe haven for countless gay teenagers who don't dare confide their sexual orientations to the people around them, it is also a very easy place to get burned. It's not just that people disappear—it's that in the end, you're never really sure who they were in the first place. And they don't really know you. Nor should they, many people say—it's just too dangerous.

"One of my main suggestions for anyone online is to come up with an alias, and use it at all times," said the adviser I spoke with. "We don't realize how much information we disclose without noticing it. A hypothetical example: 'My name is Danny, and I live in Southern Pa. outside of a large town, and play basketball. I attend PHS. Today after class I have practice, and then we are going to "Markus Theater" to watch a movie.' To show you how easy it is . . . if I were a predator . . . I would look up Markus Theater, find the location, then with a little thinking find out that PHS equals Pitts High School. Now all I have to do is find out the next basketball game, which player is Danny and that's that. . . . ALL TOO SIMPLE."

He has a point. By fostering intimate exchanges stripped of all context, Internet dialogue combines too much information with too little. The possibility of deception is implicit; Sherry Terkle, a clinical psychologist and sociology professor at M.I.T. who has written extensively about cyberrelationships, maintains that the very nature of Web interaction involves a kind of fragmentation of what we have traditionally called "identity"—a breakdown of the unified self. "In the culture of simulation," she writes in *Life on the Screen,* a book about identity and the Net, "if it works for you, it has all the reality it needs."

And that simulation, according to many, is part of the fun. "I'm not very good-looking in the real world, so why can't I lie a little in the virtual world?" asked Fred "In real life, I'm very shy and afraid to really say what I'm thinking, but online, I'm bold, and I'm also a bit more. . . . I guess the word is 'slutty.'". . .

Meeting in Real Time

It was the end of September 2000 before I finally heard back from Jeffrey. "I am terribly sorry that I have not e-mailed you," he wrote. "My relationship with C. has 'gone down the drain,' so to speak. . . . I am suffering from clinical depression." Shortly thereafter, we spoke on the phone, and I asked what had gone wrong. "I'm at a loss," he said. . . .

I proposed the idea of a visit to Jeffrey, and he immediately agreed. In early November 2000, I flew to a large Southern city and drove for several hours along an Interstate littered with blown tires and road kill before reaching Jeffrey's hometown, indistinguishable from thousands in rural America: one-story houses lining shady streets; an anemic downtown; a tentacle of roadway crammed with chain motels and fast-food restaurants clutching at the Interstate.

It was late afternoon, but as I drove to the restaurant where I'd arranged to meet Jeffrey, the sunlight felt withering. Jeffrey hovered just inside the glass door. I had imagined someone fragile and fair-skinned, but he looked nothing like that. He was nervous, and his anxiety was contagious. As we sat down at a table in the nearly empty restaurant, he explained that he had just run into a girl he knows from school. Had I walked in while he was talking to her, it would have been a catastrophe: in a town this small, no imaginable excuse could account for a high-school boy having a rendezvous with a strange woman from New York.

Mercifully, no other acquaintances of Jeffrey's appeared, and eventually we slipped into the easy dialogue we had experienced on the phone and through e-mail. . . .

Jeffrey and I left the restaurant and drove around his town in the thick, dusty light of sunset. It took all of 10 minutes. We passed his high school, where, he said, separate proms and homecomings are held for black and white kids. We joggled over train tracks into the shell of downtown. It was such a quiet place. "I feel like an alien here," Jeffrey said, and it wasn't hard to see why he lunged so heedlessly at something else, or why losing it had left him feeling empty-handed.

"At one point I felt that close to C., that I would give up my life," he said. "I would die for him. That scares me, that depth of feeling for someone you've never met."

For Gays, a Touch of Reality

Yet the very fact that Jeffrey has had this heartbreak—so characteristic of "normal" adolescence—is a remarkable change. When I spoke with Caitlin Ryan, she cited 1993 and 1996 studies that found the average age of awareness of same-sex attraction to be 10 years old. A subsequent study has found that heterosexual attraction, too, begins at this age.

"This is happening in fourth grade, regardless of sexual orientation," Ryan said. "If you repress normative sexual and psychological and psychosocial development for 10 years, that is not a healthy thing. And that's historically what happened for many lesbians and gay men." She points to unsafe sex and substance abuse as frequent consequences of that repression. "Those are some of the downsides of not being able to have a normative adolescence, not being able to go to a prom, not being able to have a boyfriend, to learn all those things that are age-appropriate when you're an adolescent."

When I spoke to Jeffrey at the end of Thanksgiving weekend, he had some news: he had managed to connect with a live human gay person, a 24-year-old man whom he drove to meet in a nearby city after first encountering him in an Internet chat room. They had dinner at a mall and shopped at the Gap and at Old Navy and at several music stores. At the end of the evening, they kissed, something Jeffrey had never done before.

"I had to do a double take," he said. "Whoa, O.K. You're gay and so am I. I'm actually here, doing this."

He expects the relationship to move slowly, and is still busy trying to meet other people. Recently he made plans to rendezvous with a fellow 16-year-old in another town. The boy planned to take Jeffrey to a coffeehouse popular with teenage gays, and Jeffrey was hugely excited. Over time, he hopes to cultivate a network of gay friends in his region.

He still thinks of C., he said, but he . . . is relieved to feel the obsession losing its hold. "There were times when I felt wonderful in the relationship with C.," he told me. But after the date—his first—he lay in bed that night and felt the difference. "It was so incredible, because it was like, I could go back and do it all over again today," he said. "And he's not just a screen name, it's not just typing and it's not just a picture. It's three-dimensional, you know? REALITY. It was awesome."

The New Generation: Gay Teen Activists

Doug Ireland

Doug Ireland writes frequently on politics for the *Nation* and is a former columnist for the *Village Voice* and the *New York Observer*. In the following article, Ireland acknowledges the continued existence of homophobia among teens, teachers, and school administrators. However, he reports, gay and lesbian teens have begun to respond in a more militant way to such discrimination. He describes the growth of teen involvement in such activist organizations as the Gay, Lesbian, and Straight Education Network (GLSEN) and the student-initiated Gay/Straight Alliances. He also notes the increase in lawsuits brought against schools by gay and lesbian teens. Nonetheless, writes Ireland, the persistent harassment faced by many gay and lesbian teens points to the need for additional legislation and more funding for effective programs for gay youth.

Jared Nayfack was 11 years old and living in the heart of conservative Orange County, California, when he told his best friend from school that he was gay—"and my friend then came out to me," says Jared. When he turned 15, Jared celebrated his birthday by coming out to his parents and closest friends. By then, he was attending a Catholic high school, and on a school-sponsored overnight field trip, Jared and his schoolmates decided to spend their free evening at the movies seeing *The Rocky Horror Picture Show*. "Some of us had decided to get all costumed up to see it, and when the teacher who was with us saw us she threw a fit: She forced me to get up in front of the other twenty-one students—many of whom I didn't know—and tell them I was gay. Most of the kids supported me, but later that evening, one of them—a lot bigger than I was; he had a black belt in martial arts—came into my hotel room and beat me up. I was a bloody mess, and he could have killed me if another student hadn't heard my screams and stopped him." Instead of punishing Jared's assailant, the school's dean suspended Jared and put him on "academic and behavioral probation." "The dean told me that even though I was forced to tell the

others that I was gay, I was at fault because I'd 'threatened the mas-
culinity' of the kid who'd beat me up," Jared recalls.

In fear, Jared transferred to a public high school, the South Orange
County High School of the Arts. "I thought I'd be safe and could be
out when I came there—after all, it was an arts program. Boy, was I
wrong. Within two weeks people were yelling 'fag' at me in the halls
and in class. I was dressed a little glam, if you will—nothing really
offensive, just a little makeup. But when I went to the principal to
complain, she did nothing about the harassment and told me that I
was 'lacking in testosterone,'" Jared explains. To fight back, Jared
and some gay and straight friends formed a club called PRIDE,
which made a twenty-five-foot-long rainbow banner to put up in
school decorated with multicolored hands and the slogan, "hands
for equality" (the banner was banned). The club also made beaded
rainbow bracelets that many students wore—"even a lot of the football players," according to Jared—but the club was forbidden by the
administration "because it didn't have anything to do with the curriculum." The harassment got worse—so bad that Jared had to leave
school two months before graduation. "I had to fight to be before I
could study," Jared explains, "but I left there feeling really let down
and like a failure—we hadn't gotten anywhere."

When he enrolled as a freshman at the University of California,
Santa Cruz, Jared says, "I was embraced by a huge and loving queer
community. They told me, 'It's OK to be angry'—that's something I
hadn't heard before." Feeling a bit burned out, for his first six months
at Santa Cruz Jared avoided gay activism—until the day he attended a
conference of gay youth. "There were kids pulling together—I just
knew I had to help out." He attended a youth training institute run
by the Gay, Lesbian and Straight Education Network (GLSEN); began
working with Gay/Straight Alliances (GSAs) at two high schools near
the university; edited and xerox-published an anthology of adolescent writings about AIDS; created a performance piece, as part of his
self-designed major in "theatrical activism," about homophobia with
a cast of seven straight boys to the hit song "Faggot" by the rock
group Korn; and now speaks to gay youth groups around the country.
Today Jared is only 18.

Homophobia Is Alive and Well

Jared's story is fairly typical of a whole new generation of lesbian and
gay adolescents: brave, tough and resilient, comfortable with their
sexual identity and coming out at earlier ages, inventing their own
organizations—and victimized by violence and harassment in their
schools. Says Rea Carey, executive director of the National Youth
Advocacy Coalition (NYAC), an alliance of local and national service
agencies working to empower gay youth: "Five or ten years ago, kids
would go to a youth service agency and say, 'I need help because I

think I'm gay.' Today, more and more they say, 'I'm gay and so what? I want friends and a place to work on the issues I care about.' Being gay is not their problem, it's their strength. These kids are coming out at 13, 14, 15, at the same age that straight people historically begin to experience their sexuality. But they are experiencing more violence because of that."

Quantifying the number of assaults on lesbian and gay youth isn't easy. In most states, gay-run Anti-Violence Projects are woefully under-funded and understaffed (when they have any staff at all), and students are rarely aware of them, according to Jeffrey Montgomery, the director of Detroit's Triangle Foundation and the spokesman for the National Association of Anti-Violence Projects. Teachers and school administra-tors most often don't report such incidents. After pressure from state governments sympathetic to the Christian right, the Clinton/Gore Administration's Centers for Disease Control removed all questions regarding sexual orientation from its national Youth Risk Behavior Sur-vey. Now the only state to include them is Massachusetts.

There, according to its most recent questioning of nearly 4,000 high school students by the Massachusetts Department of Education, kids who self-identified as gay, lesbian or bisexual were seven times more likely than other kids to have skipped school because they felt unsafe (22.2 percent versus 3.3). A 1997 study by the Vermont Depart-ment of Health found that gay kids were threatened or injured with a weapon at school three times more than straight kids (24 percent ver-sus 8). And a five-year study released in January 2000 by Washington State's Safe Schools Coalition—a partnership of 74 public and private agencies—documented 146 incidents in the state's schools, including eight gang rapes and 39 physical assaults (on average, a single gay kid is attacked by more than two offenders at once).

With the antigay crusades of the religious right and the verbal gay-bashings of politicians like Trent Lott legitimizing the demonization of homosexuals, it is hardly surprising that homophobia is alive and well among gay kids' classmates. In November 1998, a poll of 3,000 top high schoolers by *Who's Who Among American High School Students*—its twenty-ninth annual survey—found that 48 percent admitted they are prejudiced against gays, up 19 percent from the previous year (and these are, as *Who's Who* proclaims, "America's brightest students").

All this means that, as Jon Lasser, an Austin, Texas, school psychol-ogist (and heterosexual parent) who has interviewed scads of gay kids for his Ph.D. thesis, puts it, "Many have a form of post-traumatic stress syndrome that affects their schoolwork—the fear of getting hurt really shakes them up and makes it hard to concentrate."

Fighting Back

The mushrooming growth of Gay/Straight Alliances in middle and high schools in just the past few years has been the gay kids' potent response. There is strength in numbers: GSAs break the immobilizing isolation of gay students and raise their visibility, creating a mechanism to pressure school authorities into tackling harassment; educate teachers as well as other students; create the kind of solidarity among straight and gay kids that fosters resistance to bigotry and violence; provide meaningful safe-sex education; and help gay adolescents to speak and fight for themselves. The GLSEN national office has identified at least 400 GSAs, but since the GSA movement has been student-initiated and many self-starting groups are still not in touch with national gay organizations, the figure is undoubtedly much higher. There are eighty-five GLSEN chapters around the country, and while GLSEN began in 1993 primarily as an organization of teachers and other school personnel, it is making an increasing effort to include students in its organizing.

Another strategy that has frightened reluctant school administrators into steps to protect gay youth has been lawsuits by the kids themselves. The first on record was brought by a 16-year-old Ashland, Wisconsin, student, Jamie Nabozny, who in 1996 won a $900,000 judgment against school authorities who failed to prevent Nabozny's torturous harassment from seventh through eleventh grades, including beatings that put him in the hospital. As of January 2000, there are nine similar suits pending, including cases in Illinois, Washington, New Jersey, Minnesota, Missouri and several in California (one brought by the first-ever group of lesbian student plaintiffs, in the San Jose area). But as David Buckel, the Lambda Legal Defense and Education Fund's staff attorney specializing in school matters, points out, "A lot of people call and say 'I can't afford to go to court,' or 'We live in a small town and I can't put my family through that,' or 'If we sue and win it'll raise our neighbors' taxes and we'll get bricks through our window.'" (And in late December 1999, Orange County gay students filed a lawsuit against school officials, seeking to lift their ban on a GSA at El Modena High School on the grounds that the interdiction violated their First Amendment rights.)

In a civilized country, one would think, legislation to protect kids from violence and harassment in their schools should be unexceptionable. However, despite a loopy *New York Times* editorial praising the Republican Party for a kinder-and-gentler attitude toward gays, the GOP has taken the lead in opposing state-level safe-schools bills protecting gay kids. In Washington in 1999, for the second year in a row, openly gay State Representative Ed Murray—a progressive Seattle Democrat—led the fight for his bill that would have added lesbian and gay students to a law forbidding sexual and malicious harassment in the schools. "We had the votes to pass it this year in the House, which is split forty-nine to forty-nine—we had all forty-nine Democrats and picked up sixteen Republicans. But because of the tie in party membership, all House committees are co-chaired by Democrats and Republicans, and the GOP education committee co-chairman refused to let the bill out of committee. If it had been sent to the Senate, where Democrats have a majority, it would have passed."

The way in which the GOP continues to use same-sexers as a political football to advance its chances could be seen clearly in California, where Assemblywoman Sheila Kuehl (an open lesbian who co-starred in TV's *Dobie Gillis* series in the sixties) saw her Dignity for All Students Act beaten in the Assembly by one vote. GOP front groups "targeted only Democratic Latino legislators from swing districts in an unprecedented campaign-style effort," says Jennifer Richard, Kuehl's top aide. This included prayer vigils at their district offices, very sophisticated phone-banking that switched those called directly into Assembly members' offices to complain, mailings in Spanish to every Hispanic-surnamed household and full-page ads costing $8,000–$12,000 each in local papers. The mailings and ads featured photos of a white man embracing a Latino, a black man kissing a Latino and a Latino kid in a Boy Scout uniform, and called on voters to "stop the homosexual agenda," which "doesn't like the Boy Scout pledge to be morally straight." These ads were reinforced by a $30,000 radio ad blitz by the Rev. Lou Sheldon's Traditional Family Values Coalition in the targeted legislators' districts.

Despite a Youth Lobby Day that brought 700 gay students to Sacramento to support the Kuehl bill, two Latino Democrats caved in to the pressure, insuring the bill's defeat by one vote. But in a shrewd parliamentary maneuver, its supporters attached a condensed version as an amendment to an unrelated bill in the senate, which passed it— then sent it to the assembly, where it was finally approved by a six-vote margin (making California the first state to codify protections for gender-nonconforming students, who experience the most aggressive forms of harassment). Similar bills died or were defeated in 1999 in Colorado, Delaware, Illinois and Texas.

Adolescent Activists Put On the Pressure

The difference such bills can make can be seen in Massachusetts, which has had a tough and explicit law barring discrimination against and harassment of gay students since 1993, and where its implementation benefited from strong support by then-Governor William Weld (a Republican) and his advisory council on gay and lesbian issues. Massachusetts is the only state that encourages the formation of gay student support groups as a matter of policy—which is why there are now 180 GSAs in the Bay State alone. There, the state Safe Schools program is run by GLSEN under a contract with the state's Education Department, and it organizes eight regional conferences each year for students who want to start or have just started their own GSA.

There is a skein of service agencies in large cities that operate effective programs for gay youth, including peer counseling, drop-in centers, teacher training, AIDS education and assistance for victims of violence. But these programs are all dreadfully underfunded and in many places, like Texas, are denied access to the schools. Also, gay youths themselves often complain that there is a lack of support from the adult gay movement. Says Candice Clark, a 19-year-old lesbian who graduated in 1998 from a suburban Houston high school, "A lot of the older gay community here is fearful of the youth as jail-bait, since so many people think that if you're gay you're a pedophile." She also notes that the failure of Congress to pass ENDA—the Employment Non-Discrimination Act for lesbians and gays—means that adults, especially teachers, can be fired if their sexual orientation is discovered.

Richard Agostinho, 22, who founded the Connecticut youth group Queer and Active after the 1998 murder of gay university student Matthew Shepard, and who serves as one of the NYAC national board's youth members, says the local adult-led groups "are not building relationships with young people—they need to go out and recruit them and engage in mentoring of sorts. There are plenty of young people who could add emotion and power to this movement. But if a 17- or 18-year-old goes to a meeting of a local group or community center in a roomful of 30- or 40-somethings, the adults frequently fail to create an atmosphere in which the youth feel comfortable contributing. It's a problem very similar to involving people of color or anyone not traditionally represented at these tables."

The urgency of putting the problems facing gay adolescents on the agenda of every local gay organization is underscored by a study released in September 1999 by GLSEN. It showed that of nearly 500 gay students surveyed, almost half said they didn't feel safe in their schools: 90 percent reported verbal harassment, 46.5 percent had experienced sexual harassment, 27.6 percent experienced physical harassment and 13.7 percent were subjected to physical assault.

But this new generation of adolescent activists won't be ignored. For, as Jared Nayfack says, "When you do this work you open up a whole area of your heart and soul, and when you stop, you feel it deeply. Activism is addictive—you don't ever want to stop unless there's nothing left to do . . . and that will be a long time."

CHAPTER 3

TEENS AND SEXUALLY TRANSMITTED DISEASES

Contemporary Issues
Companion

Young People: At Risk for STDs

Kim Best

In the following selection, Kim Best presents recent research on young people's risk of contracting sexually transmitted diseases, both in the United States and in other nations. According to Best, teens in most parts of the world are at high risk for many STDs; for example, the highest rates of new HIV infections typically occur among adolescents. She explains that adolescents in developing countries run an especially high risk for STDs because they tend not to be well informed about sexual matters and often are physically coerced into sexual relations. However, she reports, having accurate information about STDs does not stop many young people from engaging in risky sexual behaviors. Best concludes that one of the most effective deterrents to STDs among adolescents worldwide is the acquisition of the skills and self-confidence needed to either abstain from sex or practice safe sex consistently. Best is a senior writer/editor for Family Health International in Research Triangle Park, North Carolina.

About a third of the world's 34 million HIV-positive people are between 10 and 24 years old. In most parts of the world, most new HIV infections are among adolescents, particularly among females. Notably, a substantial number of pregnant adolescents in sub-Saharan Africa are infected. Moreover, about a third of the 333 million new sexually transmitted disease (STD) cases each year—excluding HIV—occur among people younger than 25, and recent data suggest that the adolescent STD epidemic is growing, adds Dr. Willard Cates, Jr., president of Family Health International (FHI) and an expert on STDs.

"Younger people are more likely to adopt and maintain safe sexual behaviors than are older people with well-established sexual habits, making youth excellent candidates for prevention efforts," says Dr. Cates. "Reducing adolescent infections will ultimately result in fewer infections among all age groups."

However, many interrelated and complex factors that put adolescents at risk of STDs will not be changed easily or quickly. In many settings, these include poor education, unemployment and poverty.

From "Many Youth Face Grim STD Risks," by Kim Best, *Family Health International Network*, vol. 20, no. 3, 2000. Copyright © Family Health International, 2000. For more information see www.fhi.org.

Also, urbanization tends to disrupt family relationships, social networks and traditional mores, while generating more opportunity for sexual encounters.

Adolescents in some places tend to delay their sexual debut, but others begin to have sex quite early. This is important because teenagers who have an early sexual debut are more likely to have sex with high-risk partners or multiple partners and are less likely to use barrier methods of contraception such as latex condoms, which offer STD protection.

In a 1999 analysis of studies of adolescent sexual risk-taking in several developing countries, sexual debut as early as nine years was reported in Zimbabwe. In Chile, a third of young people reported having had sex before age 15. In the analysis, today's young people in Cambodia were becoming sexually active at younger ages than in the past. And in Costa Rica and Colombia, a trend among youth to have a wider repertoire of practices (anal and oral sex) was noted.

Also putting both male and female adolescents at risk of STDs is their lack of information about sexual matters, as well as STD prevention, symptoms and treatment. Approximately one quarter of some 1,000 students surveyed in Karnataka, India, mistakenly thought that a vaccine and a cure for HIV infection existed, while half of 970 secondary-school students surveyed in Nigeria did not know that HIV causes AIDS. In a survey of more than 300 U.S. college students, the majority of students knew little about human papilloma virus (HPV) infection, transmission or prevalence, although HPV infection is the most common STD in this age group and the primary cause of cervical cancer.

Risk Perception

Even when adolescents have accurate knowledge about STDs, they often do not heed warnings to reduce risky sexual behaviors. Some adolescents at high risk, for example, do not adopt safer behaviors because they incorrectly perceive their risk as low.

Familiarity with a sexual partner often leads to a perception of decreased risk. In a study from Malawi, girls perceived little risk in having sexual relations with a boy whose mother knew their family. In U.S. studies, adolescents assumed that STD prevalence among their close friends was lower than among other teens and were surprised if they became infected by a close friend. In one U.S. study of some 200 college students, inconsistent condom use was strongly associated with the belief that sexual partners were uninfected with HIV or other STDs. These beliefs were based on individuals' perceptions that they "knew" their partner's sexual history or "just knew" their partner was safe. . . .

Perceived risk can also decrease as a relationship matures. While half of the 200 U.S. college students in this study reported consistent condom use in the first month of their sexual relationships, condom use decreased as relationships progressed.

Also affecting perceived risk, says FHI's Dr. Cates, "is the tendency for adolescents in steady relationships to be more concerned about preventing pregnancy than the risk of contracting an STD. As oral contraception use increases, condom use decreases. However, dual protection against both STDs and pregnancy is best achieved by using both male condoms and effective female contraceptive methods."

Other adolescents at high risk may not adopt safer behaviors simply because they are passing through a stage of life in which risk-taking is particularly attractive. Many adolescents either feel they have nothing to lose or feel they are invulnerable and cannot lose. Others are strongly influenced by peers. As one respondent in a field study conducted in Kenya commented: "The youngsters of the new generation really look at sex like it is an 'in thing.' You know it is 'macho' now to go to bed with a woman. Even if it is going out for a social drink, you end up in the bedroom. The bottom line is that you will have sex."

Access to Condoms

To avoid acquiring STDs, adolescents need to have the skills and self-confidence to either abstain from sexual relations or to use condoms consistently and correctly.

"Even boys should learn to say 'no' to risky sex," wrote Fred Otimgu, a student at St. Joseph's College in Layibi, Uganda, in a recent issue of *Straight Talk,* a newspaper for students that encourages youth to wait to have sexual relations or to use condoms. "When I suggested to my girlfriend that we use a condom and she refused, I left her because of my fear of HIV/STDs."

Correct and consistent use of latex condoms is the most effective means of preventing STD infection among sexually active people who are at risk. In many settings, condom use among adolescents has been increasing. However, adolescents may have difficulty obtaining condoms and knowing how to use them correctly.

Most 16- to 22-year-old participants in focus group discussions held in South Africa as part of a commercial marketing initiative said they did not use condoms due to lack of availability. Most of the 78 participants simply did not have the courage to ask for condoms at pharmacies and clinics. "Many said they were tired of being told that they should not be having sex or being refused condoms because the person who is supposed to be distributing them imposed their morality on the youth," says an HIV-positive man who helped conduct the focus groups.

For this reason, he said in an interview, "condoms need to be available wherever youth gather or 'hang out.' Also, most participants reported that they would prefer to purchase their condoms from their peers or younger sales people—not someone who is old enough to be their parent. They would also prefer to get condoms from vending machines in such places as game arcades, public toilets, night clubs, music shops or Internet cafes."

Inexperience with condoms is another problem. Often unfamiliar with condoms and apt to engage in spontaneous sex, adolescents may have problems anticipating intercourse and putting on the condom in a timely manner. Peer-group pressure plays a role, either facilitating or inhibiting condom use. "Issues of image seemed to outweigh risks," says the HIV-positive man who helped conduct the South African focus groups. "If obtaining or using condoms was too embarrassing, boring or silly, they would prefer not to use them."

Girls More Vulnerable

In developing countries, up to 60 percent of new HIV infections are among 15- to 24-year-olds, with generally twice as many new infections in young women than young men. Recent studies in several African populations indicate that 15- to 19-year-old girls are five or six times more likely to be HIV-positive than boys their own age. In one area of Kenya, 22 percent of 15- to 19-year-old girls in the general population were HIV-infected, compared with just 4 percent of boys of the same age.

Similarly, the reported incidence of syphilis, gonorrhea and particularly chlamydia has been generally higher among female teenagers than among males the same age throughout 16 developed countries (the United States, Canada, and 14 in Europe). For developing countries, very little age- or sex-specific data are available for STDs other than HIV.

Why are young women more vulnerable than young men—or older women—to STD infection? In the adolescent female, a specific type of cell lining the inside of the cervical canal extends onto the outer surface of the cervix, where exposure to sexually transmitted pathogens is greater. These cells are more vulnerable to infections such as chlamydia and gonorrhea. As women age, this vulnerable tissue recedes and usually no longer extends onto the outer surface of the cervix.

Adolescent girls are also infected with HIV more often than are adolescent boys because many have sex with older men, who are more likely to be infected than adolescent men. Older men are more likely than younger men to be able to give gifts, money or favors. . . . Also, surveys show that young women are less likely than males of the same age to report condom use.

Young male adolescents also face risks. In developing countries, older men, family members or peers often encouraged young men to begin having sex, often with potentially high-risk partners: sex workers, other men or older women. In Uganda, older women appear to seek younger boys for sexual favors and, in Malawi, younger boys seek older women. In Mexico, Guatemala and Jamaica, most of young males' first sexual relationships have been reported to be with older women. In Mumbai, India, research indicated that older married women are sexual partners of some young male adolescents from the neighborhood. In addition, some young boys have sex with men. Often, relations involve unprotected anal sex, which can cause abrasions and cuts through which HIV can pass into the receptive partner's bloodstream.

In-depth interviews in Karachi, Pakistan, by a group promoting sexual health, called Aahung (an Urdu word meaning "harmony"), suggest that adolescent boys from low-income communities are at least as vulnerable to STDs as are girls. "Boys have much more freedom to experiment," said Shazia Premjee of Aahung in an interview.

"Boys also have more access to information about sex," she says, "much of which is filled with myths and misconceptions that lead to unhealthy behaviors. Unlike girls—who generally are not allowed to leave the home unaccompanied after puberty and receive guidance from older, female members of the family—boys do not talk about sexual health with adults in their households. Sexual misconceptions, therefore, are not corrected. Also, many of the boys we interviewed had had various sexual experiences with members of the same sex."

Both young men and women sell sex. But, unlike male adolescents who often become prostitutes voluntarily, girls usually do so against their wishes. In Thailand, young girls most commonly sell sex because their parents urgently need money. Young sex workers are at a higher risk of acquiring an STD than older prostitutes because they have less power to negotiate condom use with partners. The consequences can be grim. In Cambodia, for example, nearly a third of sex workers ages 13 to 19 years are infected with HIV.

Meanwhile, a substantial number of girls have sexual relations because they are physically coerced: In various populations, between a quarter and a third of young women report having experienced coerced sexual relations. The plight of the world's 100 million street children—most of whom are between 11 and 14 years old and live in the large cities of developing countries—is even more bleak. In Guatemala, 95 percent of street girls had experienced sexual abuse. In Brazil, street youth are considered to be at high risk of HIV or STDs in part because of very early sexual debut, frequently the result of coercion.

Anal intercourse presents the greatest risk of sexual HIV transmission. However, in numerous studies, heterosexuals have been found to use condoms less often for anal sex than for vaginal sex. Furthermore, a study among 800 sexually active New York City adolescents ages 13 to 21 years showed that females practicing anal sex (about 14 percent of the 483 women in the study) were less likely to use condoms with a non-steady—and potentially more risky—partner. Of young women who practiced anal intercourse, 84 percent never used condoms with steady partners, but even more—96 percent—never used condoms with casual partners.

STD Complications

STD treatment for adolescents is often inadequate for a variety of reasons, including the fact that many adolescents do not know about available services. Services may also be inaccessible because clinics are far away or have limited hours; tests and drugs may be too expensive, female adolescents may fear pelvic examinations (even though such exams may not be necessary), young people may be too embarrassed or feel too guilty to seek treatment, and health providers may be reluctant to serve adolescents. Health facilities in places as diverse as Antigua, Senegal and Thailand have been found to deny adolescents privacy and confidentiality, and staff have been rude in some places. . . .

Correct diagnosis and treatment of STDs is particularly challenging among young women, since such STDs as gonorrhea and chlamydia are often asymptomatic. Female adolescents with symptoms tend to delay seeking help, compared with older women.

Delay or lack of treatment of STDs can have serious, even fatal, consequences. Untreated STDs—particularly chlamydia and gonorrhea—can cause pelvic inflammatory disease (PID) throughout the upper genital tract. Inflammation and scarring from this infection can either block the fallopian tubes or damage the tubal lining. Long-term consequences include chronic pain, tubal infertility or life-threatening ectopic pregnancy.

Not only is PID more common among sexually active female adolescents than older sexually active women, but female adolescents are more likely to be infected again and to experience a recurrence of PID. This is because, by beginning sexual activity early, they have more time to be infected. Repeated infections increase the risk of infertility. . . .

If an STD-infected adolescent becomes pregnant, the disease can be transmitted to her fetus or infant. Bacterial vaginosis and trichomoniasis are related to preterm delivery and low-birthweight infants.

The following STDs can cause a variety of diseases in infants—gonorrhea can cause conjunctivitis, sepsis and meningitis; chlamydia can cause conjunctivitis, pneumonia, bronchiolitis and otitis media; syphilis can result in congenital syphilis and neonatal death; hepatitis B can cause hepatitis and cirrhosis; herpes simplex virus can cause disseminated, central nervous system and localized lesions; and human papilloma virus can cause laryngeal papillomatosis. HIV can cause pediatric AIDS. Up to one in every three pregnant adolescents in some settings is HIV-infected.

American Teens' Knowledge About STDs

Henry J. Kaiser Family Foundation, MTV, and *Teen People*

In March and April 1999, to gauge teen awareness of and attitudes toward sexually transmitted diseases (STDs), the California-based independent philanthropy Henry J. Kaiser Family Foundation, the MTV television network, and *Teen People* magazine surveyed four hundred fifteen- to seventeen-year-olds across the United States, focusing primarily on STDs other than AIDS. The following selection discusses the results of the survey, which revealed that most teens lack basic knowledge about the incidence, treatment, and health consequences of STDs. According to the study, teens find it difficult to talk to adults or their sexual partners about STDs, and they primarily learn the little they do know about STDs in school.

Sometimes called the nation's "hidden epidemic," sexually transmitted diseases, or STDs, are frequently silent, exhibiting no symptoms. As a result, many more Americans are estimated to be infected than know they are. In spite of their prevalence—between one in four and as many as one in two Americans is thought to have an STD at some point in their lifetime—STDs continue to be one of the least discussed health issues. This "don't ask, don't tell" policy comes at a high price. These very common diseases can have serious health consequences ranging from pain and discomfort to problems with pregnancy and infertility to heightened risk of some cancers and HIV.

Although STDs affect people of all ages, the epidemic disproportionately impacts young people. Approximately four million teens get an STD every year. Experts estimate that as many as one in three sexually experienced young people will have an STD by the age of 24. The large majority of new cases of STDs in the U.S. annually occur among people 24 years old and younger: a quarter occur among 15–19 year olds, and 42 percent among 20–24 year olds. . . .

To learn more about the issues behind this growing epidemic, the Kaiser Family Foundation, MTV, and *Teen People* surveyed 400 15 to 17 year olds nationwide about their awareness of and attitudes toward

This information was reprinted with permission of the Henry J. Kaiser Family Foundation of Menlo Park, California; MTV of New York, New York; and *Teen People* of New York, New York. The Kaiser Family Foundation is an independent health care philanthropy and is not associated with Kaiser Permanente or Kaiser Industries.

sexually transmitted diseases (STDs)—focusing primarily on STDs other than HIV/AIDS. . . .

In spite of the startling statistics, few 15 to 17 year olds say they worry about getting an STD. In fact, most who are sexually experienced consider themselves to be at little or no risk, and few have been tested. However, the survey indicates that the problem is more likely to be a lack of knowledge than lack of concern. Many teens assume because they have no symptoms or that their health care provider has never mentioned a problem or that they do not know about any of their partners having been infected that they do not need to be concerned. Only a minority of teens who reported that they knew they did not have an STD said this was because they had been tested.

Teens, like many adults, also underestimate the national incidence of STDs, and many are misinformed or uninformed about treatment options and health consequences. Even so, they rate STDs on par with teenage pregnancy and drug use as among the most urgent issues facing young people today; only HIV/AIDS, specifically, is named by more teens.

While they believe people with STDs should not feel ashamed or guilty, many also admit to mixed emotions. Teens say that they do find it more difficult to talk about issues like STDs than to actually have sex. Most sexually experienced teens in fact had not discussed the topic with either their current sexual partner—many had never talked about STDs with any sexual partner—or their health care provider. They also admit they would find it extremely difficult to tell their partners, friends, and parents if they found out they were infected.

What teens know about STDs is learned largely in school. In addition to their parents and other general information sources, such as books or health brochures, many turn to the entertainment media. Television shows, movies, and teen magazines all rated high, equal to or above health care providers.

Summary of Survey Findings

Knowledge. American teens 15–17, like adults 18–44, seriously underestimate the incidence of non-HIV STDs in the United States, and thus perhaps their own risk of infection. AIDS tops the list when teens are asked to name sexually transmitted diseases. Even the more commonplace non-HIV STDs, like gonorrhea and herpes, trail behind AIDS in mentions.

Teens' knowledge about non-HIV STDs is uneven. Most know STDs can be spread despite the absence of symptoms and that some STDs may be symptom-free for an extended period. But many are unaware about other transmission facts and most know very little about the prognosis of specific non-HIV STDs.

Sexual education courses are teens' number one source of information on STDs. Parents are a distant second. Teens who say they learned "a lot" about STDs in health class are somewhat more knowledgeable than others.

Talking with health care professionals is also beneficial. Teens who say they have gotten "a lot" of information about STDs from doctors tend to know a bit more about non-HIV STDs than other teens. Among sexually active teens, those who have talked with a health care professional about STDs are more likely to raise the subject with their sexual partners.

Attitudes. Teens evaluate their personal risk of STD infection in much the same way as adults who have never been married. Just under half feel they are not at risk at all, a third see a slight risk, and the remaining fifth see themselves at moderate or great risk. Teenage boys are more likely than teenage girls to believe they are at risk.

Teens, like adults, see STDs as a health issue with a moral dimension. If Americans had higher moral standards, according to the majority of teens, STDs would not be the problem they are today. But most teens also reject the notion that people with STDs should feel ashamed or guilty.

Most teens feel people with STD infections are obligated to tell their partners. However, teens feel less strongly about this than adults, and are less likely to recognize this responsibility if condoms are used or if the infected person only has sex when they are symptom-free.

Teens say that talking about sexual issues, like STDs, with friends, family, and sexual partners is uncomfortable. And most teens admit if they actually had an STD, telling people close to them, and their parents in particular, would be especially difficult.

Behavior. Half the teenage boys and a third of the girls surveyed say they have had sexual intercourse. Most sexually experienced teens are also sexually active; that is, they have had sex in the last 12 months. And many say they are now in a sexual relationship. Though the majority of sexually experienced teens have only had one or two partners, a minority have had three or more.

Teens practice safer sex more consistently than never-married adults. Eight in ten sexually experienced teens say they used a condom last time they had sex and over half say they always use them. Still, a notable minority of teens admit they are not using protection consistently.

As a group, teens might be more consistent condom users than adults, but they are not as consistent in discussing STD risks with partners. Less than half of sexually experienced teens discussed STD risks with their current or most recent partner.

One in four sexually experienced teens have had an HIV test and three in ten have been tested for non-HIV STDs. Teenage girls are more likely than teenage boys to have been tested for both HIV and other STDs.

Many of those teens who have been tested for non-HIV STDs are unsure what specific diseases they have been tested for. One in five cannot identify any diseases by name and one in four report being tested for "all of them." Only one in ten sexually experienced teens say they have been tested for chlamydia, the most common bacterial STD.

Teens believe that both the feeling they are not at risk and the fear of finding out they have an STD keep teenage boys from getting tested for STDs. Few feel the discomfort that may be associated with STD tests discourages testing among teen boys.

Teens Lack Knowledge About STDs

American teenagers 15–17 radically underestimate the incidence of non-HIV STDs in the U.S. today, and thus perhaps their own risk of becoming infected. Having come of age in the era of AIDS, teens often think first and foremost about AIDS when asked about STDs. Teens' familiarity with non-HIV STDs, and their knowledge about how they are spread, whether they are curable, and what their potential consequences are is uneven. They know a great deal about some aspects and very little about others.

Four in ten teens 15–17 report they have had sexual intercourse, making their lack of knowledge particularly notable. Sexually experienced teens, who arguably have the most immediate need for information about the dangers of unprotected sex, are no better informed about STDs than teens who have not yet had intercourse.

Teens 15–17 radically underestimate the incidence of non-HIV STDs, as do adults 18–44. Just one in four teens and the same number of adults know more than one in ten Americans will have an STD at some time in their life. This tendency to misjudge the prevalence of STDs exists across all demographic groups.

Teens today say they face many important health issues. Four in ten say AIDS/HIV is among the most important health issues facing teens these days. Substantial minorities of a third feel that non-HIV STDs, drug abuse, and teen pregnancy are among the most important concerns. With the exception of AIDS/HIV, teenage girls tend to be slightly more concerned about these issues than teenage boys. But even among boys almost all view these problems as serious and important threats to the health of today's teens.

Many teens think of AIDS/HIV first, and some think only of AIDS, when they talk about STDs. When asked to name specific STDs, teens name AIDS more than any other STD: almost four in ten (37%) name it first, and one in ten (11%) can name only AIDS. In comparison adults 18–44, most of whom grew up before the age of AIDS, name gonorrhea, syphilis, and herpes more frequently than AIDS, only 15% think of it first, and almost none (2%) name only AIDS.

And teens can name fewer non-HIV STDs than adults; one in three (35%) teens can name three or more compared with one in two (47%) adults. The non-HIV STDs teens mention most are gonorrhea and herpes. They are less likely than adults to name syphilis and chlamydia.

Among teens no demographic differences exist, with one exception. Teens from lower income homes are more likely to think only of HIV when asked to name sexually transmitted diseases.

Confusion About Transmission

Teens 15–17 are quite knowledgeable about some aspects of how STDs are spread, but poorly informed about others. Nine in ten teens (90%) know a person can spread an STD even if he or she has no symptoms, and a similar percentage know people with STDs may not display symptoms for months or even years after being infected (91%). Most adults 18–44 also know these basic facts.

Teenage boys and girls are equally knowledgeable about these transmission details, as are teens of different ages. Minority teens and lower-income teens are somewhat less likely to know STDs can be symptomless for long periods of time and can be spread even when symptoms are not evident, though the majority do know these important facts.

What a sizable majority of teens do not know is that during intercourse a female has a greater chance of getting an STD from a male than a male has of getting one from a female. Eight in ten teens (80%) incorrectly think it as likely for a male to get an STD from a female as vice versa. Less than two in ten (16%) teens know transmission is more likely from male to female. Adults 18–44 are slightly better informed about this transmission fact; three in ten (29%) know male to female transmission is more likely. Among teens, girls are no more likely than boys to know about their increased infection risk.

Another detail many teens are confused about is whether STD infections increase susceptibility to HIV. A substantial minority (45%) of teens are unaware that STD infections place people at greater risk of becoming infected with HIV or AIDS. Just over half (55%) of teens do know this important fact.

Teens from lower income homes (under $40,000) are more likely than those from wealthier homes to know that STDs increases susceptibility to AIDS (62% vs. 49%).

Confusion About Cures and Effects

Most American teens (89%), like most adults 18–44 (89%), know AIDS is not the only incurable STD. But beyond this basic fact, teens' knowledge about which STDs are chronic is poor. Just under half know herpes is incurable, and only three in ten know HPV is chronic. Even fewer teens know gonorrhea and chlamydia are curable. Adults are better informed about the prognosis of herpes, gonorrhea, and chlamydia, but are just as ill-informed as teens about the HPV virus.

Teenage boys and girls are equally ill-informed about the prognosis of these different diseases. Older teens, those ages 16 and 17, are more likely than 15 year olds to know herpes (51% vs. 37%) is not curable and that gonorrhea is (25% vs. 13%).

Fortunately, many teens recognize their lack of knowledge. A majority admit they do not know whether chlamydia (60%) or gonorrhea (52%) are curable, and substantial minorities admit being unsure about HPV (41%) and herpes (29%).

Teens (60%) are less aware than adults (74%) that STDs can have long-term effects on the health of women and teenage girls, and they are less informed about what these effects might be. Here too teens seem willing to acknowledge their lack of awareness; a quarter (25%) say they do not know if women with STDs face long-term health consequences. Teenage girls are more likely to know about potential effects than boys (65% vs. 55%), just as women are more aware than men (81% vs. 68%). When asked, in an open-ended format, what these consequences are, teenage girls most often cite fertility problems (35%), pregnancy and childbirth problems (18%), and cancer (7%). Teenage boys name the same problems, but do so less frequently.

Teens are also unsure whether STDs have long-term effects on males. Half of the teen boys (51%) and girls (50%) surveyed say there are such effects, and most of the remaining half (33%) say they are not sure if there are effects or not. Adults are slightly more aware that men with STDs may face future health problems (61%).

A False Sense of Confidence

American teens 15–17, like adults of reproductive age, are confident they know most of what there is to know about STDs. Eight in ten (79%) boys age 15 to 17, and even more girls (87%) say they know at least a fair amount about STDs. Girls are slightly more likely than boys to say they know "a lot." Teens from higher income homes also tend to believe they are more knowledgeable.

To some extent teens' confidence in their knowledge about STDs may be justified. Those who say they know at least a fair amount about STDs are somewhat more knowledgeable than those who admit not knowing much at all. They can name more non-HIV STDs, are somewhat more likely to know which are chronic, and are more likely to know about STDs' long-term health effects. However, they are not better informed than others about transmission facts. Those who claim to know a lot are only slightly more knowledgeable than those who say they know only a fair amount.

Most importantly, all teens, those who see themselves as knowledgeable and those who do not, radically underestimate the incidence of non-HIV STDs, and thus perhaps their risk of becoming infected.

Sources of Information About STDs

Sex education classes are teens' number one source of STD information. Eight in ten say they learned at least "a fair amount" from such classes, including half (50%) who learned "a lot." Just over half (55%) say they have learned at least a fair amount about STDs from their parents, placing parents a distant second source of information.

Beyond classes and parents, teenage boys and girls learn about STDs from different sources, and girls make greater use of many sources. Teenage girls list teen magazines as their third source; more than half of the girls (58%), and only a third as many boys (16%), have gotten information about STDs from magazines. Teen girls are also more likely to turn to parents, books or brochures, and health professionals. The only source teenage boys are more likely to turn to is girls themselves—that is, their girlfriends or sexual partners (26% vs. 18%).

Teens who say they learned a lot from these various sources tend to think they know more, but they may have a false sense of confidence. With a few exceptions, this survey provides little evidence that those who say they get a lot of information from any of these various sources are more knowledgeable. In fact, those who say they learned a lot from their parents, perhaps because parents emphasize AIDS prevention or lack knowledge themselves, are less likely to know that some other STDs are chronic (79% vs. 92%). Sources like television, friends, and boy or girl friends have little or no effect on teens' knowledge.

The good news is that some teens are evidently listening in sex education classes, and it may have paid off. Teens who say they learned a lot in sex ed. can name more non-HIV STDs than those who learned less, and are more likely to know that people with STDs may not display symptoms for some time (95% vs. 87%), that herpes is chronic (53% vs. 38%), and that gonorrhea is not chronic (30% vs. 18%). Talking with a health care professional also has some benefits. Teens who say they have gotten a lot of information about STDs from doctors can name more non-HIV STDs than those who have learned less from this source and are more likely to know that chlamydia (27% vs. 13%) and gonorrhea are curable (32% vs. 20%).

Wishful Thinking About Risk

Only one in five teens recognizes that a person puts him- or herself at risk for STD infection with just one sexual encounter. One in four thinks risk does not become significant until a person has slept with more than 20 people. . . .

Girls are more likely than boys to recognize the dangers inherent in just one sexual liaison (25% vs. 13%). Conversely, half (51%) of boys contend that significant risk does not begin until a person has had seven or more partners. Girls are less likely to believe this, although more than a third (37%) do.

Teens rate their own risk in much the same way as never-married adults age 18–44. Just under half feel they are not at risk at all (47%), a third see a slight risk (34%), and the remaining fifth see themselves at least at moderate risk (18%). Sexually experienced teens (31%) are more likely than those who have never had sex (8%) to rate their risk as moderate or great. Among sexually experienced teens, those who are now in a sexual relationship are more likely than those who are not to rate their risk moderate or great (39% vs. 25%).

Teenage boys are more likely than girls to see themselves at moderate or great risk (25% vs. 11%). Girls are twice as likely as boys to say they are not at risk at all. These gender differences exist even when sexual experience is taken into account. . . . As teen males age, their perception of their own risk increases. Only 18% of 15 and 16 year old boys think they are at moderate or great risk, compared with over a third (36%) of those age 17. Girls' perception of personal risk does not increase substantially with age.

Teens whose sexual behavior puts them in jeopardy seem somewhat aware of their increased risk. Those who have had three or more partners are twice as likely than those who have had only one or two to say their risk is moderate or great (43% vs. 22%). Still, among those who have had three or more partners, one in five (20%) denies any risk at all. Those who have had overlapping liaisons rate their risk as higher than those who have not (57% vs. 28%). And those who do not use condoms *every* time they have sex see their risk as higher than those who are consistent users (40% vs. 24%).

A Matter of Public Health or Morality?

Teens, like adults, are conflicted about STDs. While the majority tend to view STDs as a public health issue, they also see an important moral dimension. . . .

If Americans had higher moral standards, according to a large majority of teens (74%), STDs would not be the problem they are today. But at the same time, nearly as many teenagers (61%) reject the notion that people with STDs should feel ashamed or guilty.

When these two seemingly conflicting responses are examined together, we find that just three in ten teens (29%) view STDs in largely moral terms—believing higher moral standards would address the STD problem and that people with STDs should feel ashamed or guilty. For most of the remaining seven in ten teens, higher moral standards would reduce the problem at the societal level, but they oppose the notion that individuals with STDs should feel ashamed or guilty. These teens see STDs as primarily a health issue that should not carry a social stigma. . . .

Teenage girls are more likely than boys to see STDs in a moral light. They are more likely to believe higher moral standards would make STDs less problematic and less apt to believe those with STDs should not feel at all guilty or ashamed.

Sexually experienced teens are more likely than those who have not yet had intercourse to feel those with STDs should not feel guilty or ashamed (68% vs. 55%) and they are less likely to feel that a lack of morality underlies the STD problem (65% vs. 80%). Likewise, teens who feel they are personally at risk for an STD infection view STDs in a less moralistic light.

The majority of teens say if they contracted an STD they would be angry at the person who infected them. Teens, however, feel less strongly about this than adults. Two-thirds of teens say they would be angry (67%), including a third (34%) who feel this way strongly. By comparison, eight in ten adults (80%) would be angry, including fully half (53%) who feel strongly about this.

Among adults, women are more likely than men to say they would be angry at a partner who infected them, and to feel strongly about it. Among teens, girls are slightly more likely than boys to say they would be angry, but those boys who say they would be angry tend to feel more strongly about it than the girls.

Partner Notification

Most teens 15–17 feel those with STDs are obligated to tell their sexual partners about their infection, no matter what. But teens are not as unanimous in this belief as adults, and teens are more likely to see the obligation to inform decreased under certain circumstances.

Almost nine in ten teens (86%) believe a person with an STD has a great deal of responsibility to tell their partners. But only three quarters (77%) see this high level of responsibility if the infected person makes sure condoms are always used, and even fewer (67%) if sex only happens when he or she has no symptoms. Adults feel more strongly that those with STDs have a great deal of responsibility to tell their partners, and are less swayed by mitigating circumstances.

Older teens (90% of 17 year olds) are slightly more likely than younger teens (80% of 15 year olds) to say people with STDs have a great deal of responsibility to tell, but are just as likely as younger teens to see this responsibility shrink when condoms are used or sex is saved for symptom-free periods. Teens from homes with incomes of $40,000 or more are more likely than those with lower incomes to say people have a great deal of responsibility to notify partners (84% vs. 70%), even if condoms are used (73% vs. 61%) or if they abstain when they have symptoms (73% vs. 61%). Minority teens see less of a responsibility to notify partners than whites.

Teens who know STDs can be spread even when there are no symptoms are more likely than those who are not aware of this to say only having sex during symptom-free times is no excuse for not telling a partner about an STD (70% vs. 44%). Still, three in ten (30%) of those who know this feel saving sex for a "safer" time mitigates partner notification responsibility.

Although most teens believe people with STDs have an obligation to tell their sexual partner, a large majority of teenage boys (75%) and girls (76%) admit they would be somewhat or very unlikely to continue a new relationship with an infected person. Only about one in five teens (22%) say a person's STD status would have no effect on their likelihood of continuing the relationship. Most adults 18–44 share a similar view; three quarters (75%) would be hesitant to continue a new relationship with an STD infected partner.

Sexually experienced teens are less open to the idea of dating someone with an STD than those who have not yet had intercourse. Eight in ten sexually experienced teens say they would be less likely to date someone with an STD (80%), including almost half (45%) who would be a lot less likely.

Talking About Sexual Issues

Teens acknowledge that talking about sexual issues, like STDs, with friends, family, and sexual partners seems difficult and uncomfortable. And they admit if they actually had an STD telling people close to them would be especially daunting. Teens tend to be less comfortable than adults talking about sexual topics.

For many teen respondents, answers to survey questions about their comfort level in talking about sexual issues are only speculative. Very few have had conversations with sexual partners about STDs (in part because only four in ten have had intercourse). Sexually experienced teens are somewhat more open to the idea of discussing sexual topics than those who have not yet had sex, though many still balk at the idea. Among sexually experienced teens, those who have had conversations about sexual issues tend to benefit from the experience, at least as far as their comfort level with these topics is concerned.

A large majority of American teens (70%), both boys and girls, acknowledge that it is sometimes more embarrassing for couples in general to talk about sexual issues, such as STDs, than to have sex. . . . White teens (74%) and teens from homes with incomes over $40,000 (75%) are more likely to voice this opinion than minority teens (59%) and those from lower income homes (62%).

Experience makes a slight difference in teens' feelings: Three quarters of teens who have never had sex believe talking can sometimes be more embarrassing than having sex (73%). Sexually experienced teens are somewhat less likely to feel this way (66%). Among sexually experienced teens, those who have never had conversations about STDs with partners are more likely to agree with this sentiment than those who have actually had these conversations (74% vs. 60%).

Teens tend to think differently of themselves than others. When asked how comfortable they would personally be talking with a partner about STDs, six in ten teens (61%) say they would be comfortable. A sizable minority (39%) do admit, however, that they would be uncomfortable. . . .

Slightly more girls (64%) than boys (57%) say they would be comfortable talking with a partner about STDs. Teens from higher income homes ($40,000 or more) claim to be more comfortable than those from lower income homes (65% vs. 53%). Experience talking about sexual issues also appears to make a difference. Among sexually active teens, those who have talked with partners are more comfortable with the idea of these conversations than those who have not (66% vs. 55%).

Admitting to Having an STD

When asked how comfortable they would feel telling sexual partners that they in fact had an STD, a different picture emerges. Eight in ten (82%) teens 15–17 say they would feel uncomfortable telling a partner, including almost half (45%) who say they would be very uncomfortable. Telling past sexual partners is an even more upsetting prospect. Eight in ten (82%) teens say they would be uncomfortable telling their past partners, including half (52%) who say they would be very uncomfortable. Teens are even more uncomfortable than adults with prospect of telling current and former partners about an STD infection.

Teens of all demographic groups feel informing partners would be uncomfortable. Among sexually experienced teens, having talked about STDs with sexual partners does not make the specter of telling past or present partners they actually have an STD any easier.

Telling friends about an STD infection is also an uncomfortable prospect for most teens, though no more so than the prospect of telling partners. Almost half of teens 15–17 say they would be very uncomfortable telling their friends (45%). . . .

For teens, the most intimidating prospect of all is having to tell their parents about an STD infection. Almost nine in ten (86%) say they would be uncomfortable telling their parents, including seven in ten (70%) who say they would be very uncomfortable.

Some teens are especially uncomfortable with the thought of having to tell their parents they have an STD. Girls (77%) and 15 year olds (78%) are more likely to say they would find telling their parents very uncomfortable than boys (63%) and teens 16–17 (66%). This discomfort is undoubtedly magnified by the fact that by telling their parents about an STD, teens would have to acknowledge that they are sexually active, which may be especially difficult for girls and younger teens. Higher income teens are more likely than those from lower income homes to say they would be very uncomfortable in this situation (74% vs. 64%).

If teens are uncomfortable talking with their parents about STDs, it is important they have other adults to turn to. The majority of teens (58%) say they would feel comfortable asking a doctor about getting an STD test. Still a significant minority (42%) would feel ill-at-ease having such a discussion. Teens are more likely than adults 18–44 to say they would feel uncomfortable discussing STD testing with a doctor (42% vs. 31%). Sexually active teens are more likely than those who have not yet had intercourse to say they would feel comfortable talking with a doctor about testing (66% vs. 54%).

Sexually experienced teens have a mixed record of responsible sexual behavior—some say they unfailingly take all the necessary steps to protect themselves and their partners from the dangers of unprotected sex, while others admit being more haphazard. The majority have discussed the risks of STD infection with a partner, but a substantial minority have never had such a conversation. Less than half have talked about STDs with a health care professional. . . .

STD Testing

Sexually experienced teens 15–17 are less likely to have been tested for HIV/AIDS and other STDs than their adult counterparts. One in four teens have had an HIV test and one in five have had one in the last 12 months. In contrast, over half of adults 18–44 have had an HIV test and three in ten have had one recently. A similar, but less dramatic generational difference exists in terms of testing for non-HIV STDs. Sexually experienced teens are less likely to have been tested than adults, though they are just as likely to have been tested recently. Unlike adults, who are more likely to have HIV tests than tests for other STDs, teens are equally likely to have been tested for HIV and other STDs.

Sexually experienced teen girls are more likely than boys to have been tested, and tested recently, for HIV and for other STDs. . . .

Many of those teens who have been tested for non-HIV STDs are unsure what specific diseases they have been tested for. When asked, one in five (19%) cannot identify any diseases by name and even more report being tested for "all of them" (27%). Teens who can say which STDs they have been tested for most often name gonorrhea (31%), syphilis (21%), and herpes (10%). Only one in ten (10%) say they have been tested for chlamydia, the most common bacterial STD.

Most of those sexually experienced teens who say they have been tested for non-HIV STDs say they were tested in a doctor's office (61%) and most say testing was part of their routine care (63%).

When teens are asked what keeps men and boys from getting tested for STDs, teenage boys and girls, and men and women, all give the same answers: the feeling that they are not at risk, and the fear of finding out they have an STD. Fewer feel the pain that may be associated with STD tests is a barrier to testing.

STDs AND ORAL SEX

Lisa Remez

Lisa Remez is an associate editor for the bimonthly journal *Family Planning Perspectives*. In the following selection, which is adapted from an article that appeared in *Family Planning Perspectives* Remez explains that many teens mistakenly believe that they cannot contract sexually transmitted diseases through oral sex. In actuality, she writes, teens who engage in oral sex without using precautions such as condoms or dental dams are putting themselves at risk for sexually transmitted diseases, including HIV. According to Remez, herpes simplex virus, hepatitis B, gonorrhea, syphilis, and chlamydia are only a few of the other infections that can be passed through oral sex. There is a pressing need for health care professionals to increase their screening of teens for STDs contracted through oral sex, Remez concludes.

Over the past few decades, nationally representative surveys have accumulated a wealth of data on levels of adolescent sexual activity. Thanks to such surveys, we know how the proportion of 15–19-year-olds who have ever had intercourse has changed over the years. Similar data exist on age at first intercourse, most recent sexual intercourse and current contraceptive use.

Yet all of these measures focus on—or relate to the possible results of—vaginal intercourse. This is natural, given that attention to adolescent sexual activity arose initially out of concerns over the far-reaching problems associated with teenage pregnancy and childbearing. More recently, infection with sexually transmitted diseases (STDs), particularly with HIV, has fueled further public and scientific interest in teenage sexual behavior.

But to what extent does adolescent sexual activity consist of non-coital behaviors—that is, mutual masturbation, oral sex and anal intercourse—that are not linked to pregnancy but involve the risk of STDs? Some of these activities may also be precursors to vaginal intercourse. Yet, health professionals and policymakers know very little about their prevalence among teenagers. . . .

It has become increasingly clear that the narrow focus on sexual intercourse in research is missing a major component of early sexual

Reproduced with the permission of The Alan Guttmacher Institute from Lisa Remez, "Oral Sex Among Adolescents: Is It Sex or Is It Abstinence?" Family Planning Perspectives, 2000, 32(6): 298–304.

activity. There is growing evidence, although still anecdotal and amassed largely by journalists, not researchers, that adolescents might be turning to behaviors that avoid pregnancy risk but leave them vulnerable to acquisition of many STDs, including HIV.

The reports in the popular press that oral sex has become widespread among adolescents cannot be confirmed or refuted because the data to do so have never been collected. Moreover, adults do not really know what behaviors teenagers consider to be "sex" and, by the same token, what they consider to be its opposite, abstinence. All of this leaves health professionals and policymakers without the means to effectively address these issues. . . .

The first hint in the popular press of a new "trend" in sexual activity among young people appeared in an April 1997 article in the *New York Times*. That article asserted that high school students who had come of age with AIDS education considered oral sex to be a far less dangerous alternative, in both physical and emotional terms, than vaginal intercourse. By 1999, the press reports started attributing this behavior to even younger students. A July *Washington Post* article described an "unsettling new fad" in which suburban middle-school students were regularly engaging in oral sex at one another's homes, in parks and even on school grounds; this piece reported an oral sex prevalence estimate, attributed to unnamed counselors and sexual behavior researchers of "about half by the time students are in high school."

Other stories followed, such as a piece in *Talk* magazine in February 2000 that reported on interviews with 12–16-year-olds. These students set seventh grade as the starting point for oral sex, which they claimed begins considerably earlier than intercourse. By 10th grade, according to the reporter, "well over half of their classmates were involved." This article laid part of the blame on dual-career, overworked "parents who were afraid to parent," and also mentioned that young adolescents were caught between messages about AIDS and abstinence on the one hand and the saturation of the culture with sexual imagery on the other. In April 2000, another *New York Times* article on precocious sexuality quoted a Manhattan psychologist as saying "it's like a goodnight kiss to them" in a description of how seventh- and eighth-grade virgins who were saving themselves for marriage were having oral sex in the meantime because they perceived it to be safe and risk-free. . . .

How valid are these anecdotal reports? Unless and until data to verify them become available, we have only impressions to go on, and there is by no means a consensus among adolescent health professionals. Some believe the level of participation in oral sex and other noncoital behaviors is probably higher now than it was in the past, while others have a "hunch" that oral sex is no more common, just much more talked about. . . .

Oral Transmission

Experts believe that the type of oral sex practiced by young teenagers is overwhelmingly fellatio, not cunnilingus. According to Deborah Tolman, senior research scientist at the Wellesley Center for Research on Women, that distinction is paramount: "We are not fainting in the street because boys are giving girls cunnilingus. Which is not to say that girls and boys never have that experience. They probably do, and just rarely do it again for a really long time, because of how girls feel about themselves and their bodies, how boys feel about girls' bodies, and the misinformation they have about each other's bodies."

Many STDs can be transmitted by either fellatio or cunnilingus, although some are more easily passed than others. According to Penelope Hitchcock, chief of the Sexually Transmitted Diseases Branch of the National Institute of Allergy and Infectious Diseases, saliva tends to inactivate the HIV virus, so while transmission through oral intercourse is not impossible, it is relatively rare. Other viral STDs that can be transmitted orally include human papillomavirus, herpes simplex virus and hepatitis B, while gonorrhea, syphilis, chlamydia and chancroid are among the bacterial infections that can be passed through oral sex.

In the absence of survey data on the frequency of oral sex, the question arises as to whether clinicians are seeing evidence of a rise in STDs that have been acquired orally. The answer depends upon the person asked. Some say they have seen no change in STDs acquired noncoitally, while others report that they are seeing both new types of infections and new types of patients—i.e., teenagers who have not yet initiated coitus but who come in with fears and anxiety over having acquired an infection orally.

Linda Dominguez, assistant medical director of Planned Parenthood of New Mexico and a nurse practitioner with a private practice, reports that at patients' requests, she is performing more oral swabs and throat inspections now than in the past. She affirms that "I have more patients who are virgins who report to me that they are worried about STDs they may have gotten by having oral sex. There are a lot of questions and concerns about herpes, since they seem to know that there is some risk of 'top and bottom' herpes, as one of my patients put it."

Sharon Schnare, a family planning clinician and consultant in Seattle, remarks that she now sees many teenagers with oral herpes. She adds that "I have also found, though rarely, oral Condylomata acuminata [a sexually transmitted condition caused by the human papillomavirus] in teenagers." Moreover, Hitchcock states that "several studies have shown that one-third of the isolates from genital herpes cases in kids right now are HSV1 [herpes simplex virus 1, the oral strain], which suggests a significant amount of oral intercourse is going on." This suggestion is impossible to verify, however, because of the extensive crossover between the two strains. Moreover, trends are especially hard to detect because of past and current problems in the reliability of type-specific testing.

Pharyngeal gonorrhea is one STD that is definitely acquired through oral sex. A few cases of pharyngeal gonorrhea have been diagnosed in adolescent girls in Dominguez's family planning clinic in New Mexico and in one region of Georgia through a community screening project among middle-school students to detect certain strains of meningitis bacteria carried in the throat. In Georgia, the cases caught everyone off guard, according to Kathleen Toomey, director of the Division of Public Health in Georgia's Department of Human Resources. The infections were found only because throat swabs were being done for meningitis in a population that would not be considered "sexually active" in the traditional sense of the word.

Teenagers Are Misinformed About Risks

Many researchers and clinicians believe that young adolescents who are having oral sex before they start coitus might be especially reluctant to seek clinical care. Moreover, adolescents virtually never use condoms or dental dams to protect against STD infection during oral sex, even those who know about the risk and worry that they might become infected.

However little is known about teenagers' experiences with oral sex, even less information is available on their involvement with anal sex, which also carries risks of STD infection, particularly of HIV. While teenage patients now seem much more comfortable talking about oral sex than they were in the past, the taboo against bringing up anal sex is still very much in place.

Experts say there are multiple, interrelated reasons for why adolescents might be turning to oral sex. Deborah Roffman, a sexuality educator at The Park School in Baltimore, asserts that "middle-school girls sometimes look at oral sex as an absolute bargain—you don't get pregnant, they think you don't get diseases, you're still a virgin and you're in control since it's something that they can do to boys (whereas sex is almost always described as something boys do to girls).". . .

Teenagers seem to be especially misinformed about the STD risks of oral sex. Experts repeatedly mentioned their concerns over adolescents' perceptions of oral sex as less risky than intercourse, especially in the context of teenagers' tendency to have very short-term relationships. Several observers mentioned the trap of AIDS education, which often teaches that HIV is transmitted through sexual intercourse, so adolescents think they are avoiding risk by avoiding sexual intercourse. Sarah Brown, director of the National Campaign to Prevent Teen Pregnancy, suggests what some adolescents might be thinking: "Okay, we get it. You adults really don't want us to have sexual intercourse, and you're probably right because of AIDS and pregnancy. But we're still sexual and we're going to do other things.". . .

There is widespread agreement that oral STD risk in adolescent populations has yet to be adequately measured and screened for. This situation is exacerbated by the fact that many of the adolescent patients involved have not yet initiated coitus and thus are unlikely to visit a family planning or STD clinic. When they do, several practitioners assert, more detailed sexual histories, despite the extra time involved, are essential to prevent misdiagnosis and to understand what the patient, rather than the provider, means by "sexual activity." In the absence of an adequate screening protocol, unknowing clinicians might automatically assume that the patient has strep and prescribe antibiotics. The fact that many infections are asymptomatic further complicates the diagnosis when the mode of infection is not easily talked about.

The deeply rooted tendency to define sex as intercourse might not necessarily be working any more in reaching many adolescent patients at risk. How to counsel adolescents about lowering that risk is especially problematic, since many young people consider oral sex itself to be a form of risk reduction and are probably already reluctant (as are many adults) to discuss oral sex openly or to use dental dams or condoms. Many practitioners feel they have gotten very good at talking about penetrative risk, but that they now need to hone their skills at communicating with their young clients about other types of sexual activities—and to do so they need more information.

Qualitative and quantitative data on sexual behaviors other than intercourse are clearly needed to close the gaps in knowledge about practices that may expose young people to emotional and physical harm. Surveys have not yet been undertaken that would yield more useful data on the broad range of sexual behaviors young people might be engaging in. If such surveys are conducted and reveal that only a small percentage of adolescents are involved, "then we need not be alarmed," according to Laura Stepp, the *Washington Post* reporter who wrote some of the first stories on oral sex. "But if it's a considerable proportion, then we need to get out there with megaphones."

CHAPTER 4

THE DEBATE OVER SEXUAL EDUCATION

THE DILEMMA OF WHAT TO TEACH IN SEX EDUCATION

Helen Lippman

In the following selection, freelance health care writer Helen Lippman focuses on the status of sex education in American schools as determined by the findings of two major studies released in 1999. Lippman reports that all but two states have accepted federal funds earmarked for abstinence-only sex education. However, she writes, many school districts teach abstinence-plus, which involves talking to students about contraceptives and safe sex while advising them that the preferred option is to abstain from sexual activity until marriage. Other schools offer a more comprehensive approach, she notes, including specific information on obtaining and using birth control. Based on the findings of the two studies, Lippman concludes that the type of sex education that students receive depends primarily on the geographic location of their school, with school districts in the South being the most likely to stress abstinence-only education.

Two recent studies look at the growing popularity—and regional variations—of "abstinence only" policies in the public schools.

For a third of our nation's public school children, sex education focuses on a single theme: No sex outside of marriage. Period. Some of these children hear about contraception in class, but only in terms of its ineffectiveness in preventing pregnancy and sexually transmitted diseases. Others don't hear about it at all—at least not in a classroom setting. That's the word from a recent Alan Guttmacher Institute study published in the November/December 1999 issue of *Family Planning Perspectives*, the official publication of Planned Parenthood. The study, conducted in 1998, is the first nationwide look at sex ed policies at the school district level.

A similar study by the Kaiser Family Foundation, conducted in 1999 and released at year's end, echoes those findings. Nearly two-fifths of middle school and junior and senior high principals report that "abstinence only" is their schools' main message. Although the

Guttmacher researchers focused on data from school districts while the Kaiser report surveyed school principals directly, the two studies came to similar conclusions. Together, they give us our first real look at how the "abstinence" philosophy has transformed sex education in the schools.

It all started in 1996, when Congress (as part of a welfare reform measure) established a $250 million, five-year fund to support state educational efforts aimed exclusively at promoting abstinence until marriage. Every state but two, California and New Hampshire, has accepted the funds. A study by the Sexuality Information and Education Council of the United States (SIECUS) predicted in 1999 that, by the end of 2002, state and federal governments will have spent nearly half a billion dollars on abstinence-only education.

Abstinence, Birth Control, or Both?

Advising students to abstain from sexual activity and talking to them about contraceptives are not necessarily mutually exclusive. In fact, 58 percent of the principals surveyed by Kaiser describe their sex ed programs as "comprehensive," based on the researchers' definition: "Young people should wait to have sex, but if they do not, they should use birth control and practice safer sex."

The Guttmacher survey also finds that a majority of public school children—54 percent—attend schools that combine the two approaches, albeit to varying degrees. Unlike the Kaiser team, the Guttmacher researchers divided the abstinence/contraception classifications into two categories: comprehensive and abstinence-plus. Only 9 percent of students are in districts that meet the Guttmacher team's definition of "comprehensive" sex ed: treating abstinence as one option in a broader sex ed program. But 45 percent are in districts with abstinence-plus policies, which "treat abstinence as the preferred option for adolescents, but also permit discussion about contraception as an effective means of protecting against unintended pregnancy and disease."

Because of variations in enrollment, statistics based on the number of school districts and those based on the number of students don't equate. While 69 percent of school districts have specific sex education policies, for example, those districts collectively enroll 86 percent of public school kids; conversely, the 31 percent with no official policy (each school, or each teacher, makes decisions about sex ed instead) represent the remaining 14 percent. Among districts with sex ed policies, 14 percent have comprehensive programs, 51 percent teach abstinence-plus, and 35 percent teach abstinence-only.

Contrary to what you might expect, small districts—those with fewer than 15,000 students—are less likely than their medium or large counterparts to teach abstinence-only. Less surprisingly, when it comes to sex education, geographical location is more telling than whether a district is in a metropolitan, suburban, or rural area. In the Northeast, for instance, abstinence is the main message in just 20 percent of the districts with sex ed programs, compared with 55 percent of Southern districts.

Guttmacher researchers David J. Landry, Lisa Kaeser, and Cory L. Richards note that "while a growing number of US public school districts have made abstinence education a part of their curriculum, two-thirds of districts allow at least some positive discussion of contraception to occur." At the same time, the researchers found that one district in three "forbids dissemination of any positive information about contraception, regardless of whether their students are sexually active or at risk of pregnancy or disease."

Landry, Kaeser, and Richards cite a study documenting public approval of access to birth control for sexually active young people—and numerous studies showing that most adults favor sex education programs. Few existing studies, the researchers note, show the abstinence-only approach to be effective in delaying young people's sexual initiation. At the same time, they point to "the growing weight of evidence" that comprehensive programs are most effective in discouraging sexual experimentation among youths and promoting contraceptive use when sexual activity begins.

A close look at the Kaiser study, however, raises questions about how far-ranging some "comprehensive" curricula really are. Nearly six in 10 principals apply that label to their school programs, but advising sexually active students to use contraception is different from providing specific details about condoms and other methods. Just 45 percent say their programs include information on how to use—and obtain—birth control, and only 39 percent cover the how-tos of condom use.

Influencing Policy

How is sex education policy determined within a school district? In the Guttmacher study, nearly half the districts with specific policies identify state directives as most influential. Much less influential are special school board advisory committees and school board actions, at just 18 and 17 percent, respectively.

When asked about factors with any influence, three out of four cite state directives, close to two-thirds name board action, and more than a third point to special committees. Teacher and community support for abstinence—together named by about a third of the districts— plays a significant role; another third say that educators and municipal leaders advocate a broader approach. According to the respondents, in more than half the districts with specific policies the community is "generally silent" about sex education.

Nearly nine Kaiser respondents in 10 say that "local government or school district" wields "some" or considerable influence, and three out of four say their sex education teachers use standard materials provided by the district. Seven in 10 say the same about state government. Asked about decisions regarding the content of the school's sex ed curriculum, 88 percent of the principals say teachers are somewhat or very involved; 72 percent point to school board or school administrators, 68 percent say parents are involved. Fifty-four percent of the principals say they themselves have participated in such decisions, but only 20 percent identify local politicians as being somewhat or very involved.

Abstinence-only sex education may be a hot political topic, but it's still not the choice of most schools, the Kaiser Family Foundation concludes. While districts with recent policy changes have been more likely to embrace rather than reject a curriculum that stresses abstinence, the Guttmacher researchers add, most choose to focus on abstinence-plus rather than abstinence-only.

ABSTINENCE-FOCUSED EDUCATION IS NOT EFFECTIVE

Deborah L. Shelton

Many supporters of abstinence-only sex education programs maintain that this approach will prevent teens from engaging in risky sexual behaviors. However, as Deborah L. Shelton reports in the following selection, the American Medical Association Council on Scientific Affairs concluded in 1999 that the effectiveness of abstinence-only programs has not been proven. Abstinence-only education is the sole option available to students in most U.S. schools, Shelton explains, yet it neglects to cover essential information vital for teens' health and safety. According to Shelton, many experts believe that students would derive greater benefit from more comprehensive programs that include accurate information about contraception and other controversial issues, such as abortion and sexual orientation. Shelton covers health and science issues for *American Medical News*.

Comprehensive sex education programs are few. In many school districts, discussion about contraceptives is prohibited or the information that's provided about them is inaccurate.

Abstinence-Only Policies Prevail

Of the seven in 10 public school districts nationwide with policies mandating sexuality education, 86% require that abstinence be taught as either the preferred option or as the only option for birth control outside of marriage, according to a recent survey by the Alan Guttmacher Institute, a nonprofit corporation that conducts reproductive health research and policy analysis.

Only 14% of school districts had a comprehensive sex education policy that included discussion of contraceptives as one way to avoid pregnancy and sexually transmitted diseases.

The survey of a nationally representative sample of 825 school district superintendents found that one-third of districts with an abstinence-only policy prohibited discussion about contraceptives or limited information about them to their failure rates in preventing unplanned pregnancy and transmission of STDs.

The Guttmacher survey was one of two recently released studies that assessed abstinence programs in public schools—the first such nationwide assessments.

The second survey polled a nationally representative sample of 313 principals of public secondary (middle, junior high and high) schools and was conducted by the Henry J. Kaiser Family Foundation, an independent health care philanthropy. It found 94% of large secondary schools discussed abstinence, but fewer than half provided information about where to get and how to use birth control. Half of the schools didn't discuss controversial topics such as abortion and sexual orientation.

Fifty-eight percent of principals described their schools' sexual education program as being comprehensive; a third said their programs taught abstinence-only.

"We are concerned about the high numbers of young people who go to school with policies that restrict the information they get about sexuality, information that could potentially be life-saving to them at some point in their lives," said Monica Rodriquez, director of information and education at the Sexuality Information and Education Council of the United States.

In December 1999 at its Interim Meeting, the American Medical Association (AMA) House of Delegates accepted without rancor a report by the Council on Scientific Affairs (CSA) that calls for comprehensive sex education. The council's report concluded that abstinence-only programs are of very limited value and require additional, rigorous evaluation before they can be supported as a method for changing students' risky practices.

"What we found is that abstinence-only programs have been poorly studied," said Nancy Nielsen, MD, PhD, a CSA member. "There's no evidence of efficacy."

Instead, the AMA urged schools to implement comprehensive, developmentally appropriate sex education programs at all levels.

Of the 69% of school districts that mandate sex education, 51% teach abstinence as the preferred option for teens but allow discussion about contraception as an effective means of preventing pregnancy and STDs, according to the Guttmacher survey. Such programs are referred to as "abstinence-plus."

Another 35% of school districts—23% of all districts nationwide—teach abstinence as the only option for birth control, and discussion of contraception is either prohibited or limited to the failure rates of particular methods.

The Number of Abstinence-Only Programs Soars

School districts in the Southern states were almost five times as likely as those in the Northeast to have an abstinence-only policy.

"We were shocked by the percentage of school districts offering abstinence-only sexuality education," said David J. Landry, senior research associate at the Guttmacher Institute and study co-author. "That's rather troubling in that accurate information about contraceptives is being withheld from students, many of whom desperately need this information to avoid pregnancy and STDs."

Particularly disturbing is that "about 50% of school districts in the South have abstinence-only policies when some of the highest rates of STDs and teen pregnancy occur in the South," Rodriquez said. "Clearly young people are having intercourse, yet many of them go to schools where they are not getting information about contraception."

The Guttmacher survey reported an increase in school programs focusing on abstinence. Of districts that changed their policies in recent years, there was a 37% decline in the number of comprehensive programs and a 22% increase in programs that taught abstinence as the preferred option.

Legislation passed in 1996 allocated $250 million in federal funds for abstinence-until-marriage programs for fiscal years 1998 through 2002. State matching funds could boost the total available monies to almost $500 million. All but two states have accepted the funds and are in various stages of implementing programs.

Teens Need Facts

Noting that 51% of women 15 to 19 years old and even more boys in that age group have already had sexual intercourse, Landry said "the principal problem of abstinence-only programs is that students who don't adhere to that message are essentially lost and receive no information about how they can protect themselves, especially if the only information they receive about the effectiveness of contraceptives is negative."

Comprehensive school-based sexuality education should be appropriate to young people's age, developmental level and cultural background and cover a wide range of topics in six key areas: human development, relationships, personal skills, sexual behavior, sexual health and society and culture, Rodriquez said.

Teenagers are looking for credible sources of information about sexuality, said Tina Hoff, director of public health information and communication for the Kaiser Foundation. But they aren't getting that information from their doctors.

A 1997 Kaiser survey, conducted with a teen magazine, of 13- to 18-year-olds found that peers were the primary source of information about sexual health issues (61%), followed by sex education classes (44%), a TV program or movie (40%), a teen magazine (39%) and parents (32%). "Doctors didn't even register," Hoff said.

"It's very important for physicians dealing with adolescents to know that young people are looking for accurate information about contraception, safe sex and HIV, in particular," she said. "There's a role that physicians can play in talking to them about these issues; this includes those who are sexually active and those who are not."

Landry said students get so little information, even in school-based programs, that it's important for pediatricians and generalists to assess their risks for pregnancy and STD.

"One-third of school districts aren't even covering information about contraception and, in many cases, it may be inaccurate," he said. Some abstinence-only programs, for example, have distributed information stating that HIV can pass through latex condoms. "Even though they've been told that that is absolutely false, they continue to disseminate it," Landry said.

THE PROBLEMS WITH ABSTINENCE-ONLY SEX EDUCATION

Sue Alford

Sue Alford is the editor and director of public information services for Advocates for Youth, an organization devoted to helping young people make safe and responsible decisions about sex. In the following article, Alford lists what she believes are serious problems with the abstinence-only sexual education requirements mandated by federal legislation in the late 1990s. Abstinence-only education jeopardizes the health and lives of young people by not informing them about how to avoid pregnancy and sexually transmitted diseases and by presenting medically inaccurate information, Alford contends. To assume that not teaching young people about safe sex will keep them from having sexual intercourse is simply naive, she asserts. Alford accuses supporters of abstinence-only-until-marriage programs of refusing to accept the reality of the world in which today's young people live—a world in which sexual expression has become the norm rather than the exception.

1. Federally mandated abstinence-only-until-marriage education jeopardizes the health and lives of young people by denying them information that can prevent unintended pregnancy and infection with sexually transmitted diseases (STDs), including HIV.

Youth need to know how to avoid the potential negative consequences of sexual intercourse. Every young person urgently needs accurate information about contraception and condoms. STDs and unintended pregnancy are extremely common. Consider the following:

- One-half of all new HIV infections occur among people ages 25 or less.
- One-quarter of all new HIV infections occur among people under age 21.
- The human papilloma virus—genital warts—is so common that experts believe three-quarters of *all* the sexually active people in the world have been infected with it.
- In the 1995 National Survey of Family Growth, 28 percent of *all*

From "What's Wrong with Federal Abstinence-Only-Until-Marriage Requirements?" by Sue Alford, *Transitions*, March 2001. Used with permission.

women reported having had an unintended birth, and one-fifth of those women reported the birth as unwanted.

2. Proponents of abstinence-only-until-marriage education assume that, if young people do not learn about contraception, they will not have sexual intercourse.

Throughout human history, people have had sexual intercourse. Often, people had to rely on contraceptive methods that were not very effective in preventing unwanted pregnancy because highly effective methods were not available. Today, highly effective methods are available to help people avoid unintended pregnancy, if they know about these methods and have access to them.

The fact that some U.S. teens report oral and/or anal intercourse while considering themselves "virgins" underscores the fact that lacking information does not prevent young people from having sexual intercourse. It may, however, prevent them from making healthy choices about sexuality.

However, abstinence-only-until-marriage education goes further. It discourages young people from using contraception. It encourages young people to believe that condoms and modern methods of contraception—such as birth control pills, injectable contraception, implants, and the intra-uterine device (IUD)—are far less effective than they, in fact, are. Many abstinence-only-until-marriage programs discuss modern methods of contraception only in terms of failure rates (often exaggerated) and censor information about their correct use and effectiveness. Thus, many of these programs keep young people in ignorance of the very facts that would encourage them to protect themselves when they eventually become sexually active.

- By age 18, about 71 percent of U.S. youth have had sexual intercourse.
- One recent study found that, by the age of 18, more than 75 percent of young people have engaged in various heavy petting behaviors.
- Another study found that 25 to 50 percent of teens report having had oral sex.
- A third study focusing exclusively on adolescent "virgins" (defined in the study as teens who had not experienced vaginal intercourse) found that nearly one-third of respondents reported having participated in masturbation with a partner. In the same study, 10 percent of teens who defined themselves as virgins had participated in oral intercourse and one percent had participated in anal intercourse.
- Data from a nationally representative survey indicate that, in 1999, 49.9 percent of all high school students have had sexual intercourse. The percentage rises by grade level—38.6 percent of ninth graders have had sexual intercourse compared with 64.9 percent of seniors.

- By the time young people reach age 20, about 80 percent of
  males and 76 percent of females have had sexual intercourse.

Federal legislation does not define sexual activity when it requires
sexuality education classes to teach that "abstinence from sexual activity outside of marriage is the expected standard for all school-age children." Holding hands, kissing, deep kissing, petting—each of these
may be included in the disapproved category of "sexual activity" in
individual abstinence-only-until-marriage curricula. At the same time,
these curricula provide no guidance about very real behaviors that put
youth at risk—oral and/or anal intercourse. Yet, the reality is that
almost every American teenager today has had at least one romantic
relationship by the time he/she is 18, and most young people have
engaged in "sexual activity." In fact, most American parents would be
likely to worry about the well-being of a teenager who went through
his/her entire teenage years without even one romantic relationship.

If these young people have had abstinence-only-until-marriage sexuality education, they will not know how to protect themselves and
their partners from STDs and unintended pregnancy. In the end,
research demonstrates that, instead of keeping young people from
having sexual intercourse, abstinence-only-until-marriage programs
merely keep them from having safer sexual intercourse.

*3. Federal requirements assume that young people will not learn about
sexuality from any source other than sexuality education classes.*

Legislators and congressional staff do not acknowledge the world
in which young people live. If they did, they would hesitate to push,
as an ultimate value, something that is actually a norm. Moreover, it
is a norm that is contradicted by nearly every television show, movie,
popular magazine, song, or music video that young people see, hear,
or read. This legislatively mandated norm is contrary to the behaviors
of many adults (including members of Congress and their staff) that
young people hear or read about. Young people learn about sexual
expression nearly everywhere they turn in society. They do not learn
about responsible, mutually respectful, sexual expression in many
places—and certainly not in abstinence-only-until-marriage programs. In such programs, they learn instead about a single congres-
sionally mandated standard that is at odds with nearly every other
sexuality message they receive from the society in which they live.

Federally funded abstinence-only-until-marriage programs must
teach that "a mutually faithful monogamous relationship in the context of marriage is the expected standard of human sexual activity." By
contrast, a recent nationally representative poll found that 56 percent
of U.S. adults agreed that sexual intercourse should be reserved for a
committed, monogamous relationship, *whether or not* people are married. Only 33 percent believed that sexual intercourse should occur
only within marriage. Moreover, 93 percent of men and 79 percent of
women report having had sexual intercourse prior to marriage.

The refusal of abstinence-only-until-marriage proponents to accept the reality of young people's lives also creates a vacuum for youth as to what constitutes "sexual activity." Indications are emerging that many youth engage in unprotected sexual activities, such as oral and anal intercourse, while avoiding coitus (vaginal-penile intercourse). Abstinence-only-until-marriage programs cannot even address these issues because they shrink from discussing specific sexual behaviors.

A Matter of Core Values

Comprehensive sexuality education rests upon certain core values, including
- Every individual has dignity and self-worth.
- Sexual relationships should never be coercive or exploitative.
- All sexual decisions have effects or consequences.
- Every person has the right and the obligation to make responsible sexual choices.

Comprehensive sexuality education encourages young people to complement these values with the values of their parents, society, and culture and to define and clarify the values by which they can live fulfilling, satisfying lives. Comprehensive sexuality education does not supplant family values; rather, it provides young people with the tools to integrate these values into their lives and daily decision-making.

When a teen identifies his/her own values and the norms that are consonant with those values, that teen is unlikely to fall back on doing something because "everyone is doing it" or to engage in activities just to circumvent an arbitrarily imposed standard. A vital developmental component in comprehensive sexuality education is encouraging teens to think and teaching them *how* to think rather than *what* to think. It is a component that is missing in abstinence-only-until-marriage education, which prefers to tell teens *what* to think and distrusts their ability to think for themselves.

4. Federally funded abstinence-only-until-marriage education too often provides young people with medically inaccurate information.

Abstinence-only-until-marriage education provides no information about contraception and condoms other than failure rates. Moreover, it often provides inaccurate information, even about failure rates. In asserting that condoms are ineffective, abstinence-only-until-marriage education usually relies on studies that either pre-date today's highly effective latex condoms or that are not scientific in their research and analysis and, thus, are not published in peer-reviewed journals. Another tactic of proponents of abstinence-only-until-marriage education is to link condom failure with sexually transmitted infections that may occur in areas of the body that condoms do not cover and, thus, *could not* protect. For example, recent abstinence-only arguments against using the condom to prevent HIV infection have focused on the inability of condoms to protect one totally against human papillomavirus (genital warts). What opponents fail to mention, however, is that genital warts may be transmitted across portions of the anatomy (such as the upper thighs, lower abdomen, the groin, testicles, labia majora, or anus) that condoms do not cover.

Second, federal guidelines require abstinence-only-until-marriage programs to teach that "sexual activity outside of marriage is likely to have harmful psychological and physical effects." First, consider the assertion about harmful physical effects of sexual activity outside of marriage. Certainly, sexual intercourse can result in unplanned pregnancy, STDs, and/or HIV infection. But these results are not necessarily "likely." Moreover, these negative physical consequences are not linked to marital status and may occur inside or outside of marriage. It is precisely to protect against negative physical consequences that comprehensive sexuality education provides young people with information on contraception and condoms.

Next, consider the claim about negative psychological effects of sexual activity outside of marriage. There is simply no sound public health or medical data to support this assertion. Most people have had sexual relations prior to marriage with absolutely no negative psychological consequences. For example, one study reported that, when premarital sexual intercourse is satisfying, it positively affects the relationship for both males and females. The largest study ever undertaken of adult sexual behavior found that more than 90 percent of men and more than 70 percent of women recall wanting their first sexual intercourse to happen when it did.

Sexuality is a natural, normal, and positive component of life. Comprehensive sexuality education can address issues in a positive, helpful manner that encourages young people to make responsible and safe decisions that protect their sexual health.

MAKING A CASE FOR ABSTINENCE-ONLY SEX EDUCATION

Alice Seagren

In 1996, the U.S. Congress enacted legislation allocating several million dollars for the development of sex education programs that teach abstinence as the only option for unmarried teens. In the following selection, Minnesota State Representative Alice Seagren explains her reasons for supporting this controversial legislation. Most parents want their school-age children to remain abstinent, Seagren contends, and the educational system should establish these same sexual standards instead of undermining parental authority. In Seagren's view, sex education that encompasses the teaching of safe sex fails to stress the consequences of premarital sex and promotes promiscuity. Teens who learn abstinence-based resistence skills are more confident, higher achievers, and less likely to engage in risky behaviors than teens who are not taught that abstinence until marriage is the only acceptable standard, she concludes.

Controversy continues in Minnesota and elsewhere over a tiny component of the 1996 welfare reform bill designed to prevent out-of-wedlock births. Under the legislation, $250 million will be spent over five years to help states develop abstinence-only sex education programs. Designed to reduce single-parent welfare caseloads, the new law has reignited a decades-old controversy: What should we teach our children about sex?

Complying with the Law

The abstinence-only sex education law has a single goal: to actively discourage premarital sex among adolescents because single-parent households have the greatest hurdles to overcome in leaving the welfare system.

Eighty percent of teen mothers end up in poverty, and these young mothers are less likely to finish school. Inadequate support from non-resident fathers makes it extremely difficult for these teens

Reprinted from "Making the Case for Abstinence-Only Sex Education," Alice Seagren, *Saint Paul* (Minnesota) *Legal Ledger*, February 3, 1998, with permission.

to provide for their children. During a teen mother's first 13 years of parenthood, she will earn approximately $5,600 a year, less than half the poverty level.

Minnesota's abstinence-only sex education proposal received federal funding approval in 1997.

But Minnesota's and other states' proposals have raised concerns among members of Congress because they do not fully comply with the new law. In October 1997, the National Coalition for Abstinence Education gave Minnesota's plan a failing grade because it failed to emphasize the mandated standard of "abstinence until marriage" and because it focused on youth 14 and under and not on teens in the 15-and-above age group where abstinence education may be most needed. . . .

The new abstinence-only law requires participating states to instruct youths that sex outside of marriage can have harmful psychological and physical effects and that sexual abstinence is the expected standard for all school-age children. The new law also prohibits using abstinence funds to promote or distribute contraceptives to youths.

Teens Receive a Mixed Message

The law is controversial because it challenges the very underpinnings of contemporary sexual education curricula that explicitly tutors teens, "You're sexual beings. Explore. Do it. Just make sure you wear a condom."

Today's sex ed curricula is at odds with itself. It teaches children to postpone sexual involvement and arms them with resistance skills. But at the same time, in teaching the dangers of sexually transmitted diseases, the curriculum places a premium on "protected sex" and contraceptive use.

At its best, it sends teens a mixed message. At its worst, it unwittingly condones promiscuity. It is a failed strategy because it does not set a clear standard that engaging in premarital sex has enormous consequences.

In 1996, U.S. Health & Human Services Secretary Donna Shalala hailed news that the long-term increase in teenage sexual activity had finally declined after three decades of growth. The 1995 National Survey of Family Growth found that the percentage of women aged 15–19 having sexual intercourse dropped to 50 percent from 55 percent in 1990. The rate had climbed from 29 percent in 1970.

Good news? Yes, but as parents, shouldn't we be dismayed that we're celebrating the fact that only 50 percent of our teenage daughters are having sexual intercourse?

Abstinence Is the Only Option

To many, sexual abstinence must seem like both a naive and repressive doctrine in our sex-obsessed culture. Teaching young men and women to abstain from sex until marriage seems hopelessly anachronistic when television and other media constantly reinforce the widespread notion that promiscuity is acceptable because "everyone does it."

However, whether for moral, psychological or physical health reasons, most parents disapprove of their teen-aged sons and daughters engaging in premarital sex.

A 1997 University of Minnesota study about risky adolescent behavior showed that such disapproval can be effective in protecting teens from early sexual involvement and pregnancy. It showed that children are less likely to have early intercourse if parents provide a clear message about delaying sex. But current sex education, which validates promiscuity under the rubric of safe sex, knowingly undermines that parental authority.

Teaching teens AIDS awareness, giving them the skills to resist sexual pressure and setting a standard of abstinence can be an effective method to help them postpone sexual activity. Young people armed with abstinence-based resistance skills are more confident, have greater self-esteem, are less likely to engage in other risky behaviors and become better achievers.

Abstinence from premarital sex is the expected standard most parents set for their school-age children. Why isn't it the clearly stated standard in our schools?

The overwhelming approval of abstinence-only sexual education in the federal welfare bill was significant. Even though the one-time allocation pales to the $200 million spent every year for family planning under the Public Health Service Act, the abstinence-only law signals a long-overdue correction in public policy.

THE GROWTH IN SUPPORT FOR ABSTINENCE-FOCUSED EDUCATION

Ken Walker

In the following selection, *Baptist Press* writer Ken Walker reports on the growing trend toward abstinence-only sex education. He cites the success of several abstinence-based programs, such as True Love Waits and Project Save Our Students (SOS). The number of groups promoting abstinence increased tenfold between 1992 and 1997, Walker relates, and many parents support the inclusion of abstinence-only programs in mainstream public education. The passage of legislation providing federal funding for abstinence education has also given these programs added legitimacy, Walker notes. Furthermore, he states, teens are increasingly receptive to the abstinence-only message, which reassures them that they do not have to rush into adult decisions about sex that they are not yet ready to make.

After five years of fighting values-free sex education curriculum, Joneen Krauth believes the tide is turning in favor of abstinence.

"It is awesome," said Krauth, a former intensive care nurse who teaches public school workshops known as WAIT Training, which stands for "Why am I Tempted?"

Krauth, of suburban Denver, Colorado, organized the seminars after reviewing her son's seventh-grade science text and finding a unit included instruction in condom use.

In north Florida, former teacher Pam Mullarkey is seeing similar success in reaching teen-agers. The founder of Project Save Our Students, or SOS, said her abstinence-based program has made presentations to 10,000 students in five counties. It also is beginning new works at a juvenile institution and the U.S. Naval Station at Jacksonville, Florida.

Mullarkey, who organized SOS after hearing about a 14-year-old student's abortion, said many people lacking personal restraint are also heavily in debt.

"They have a lack of self-control in spending, as well as with alcohol, drugs and sex," she said. "We're teaching people self-control and how to run their lives by goals, not by their emotions."

From "Pro-Abstinence Groups Show Tenfold Growth," by Ken Walker, *Baptist Standard*, December 17, 1997. Reprinted with permission.

Congress Provides Legitimacy

Initiatives such as WAIT Training and SOS underscore key gains by the pro-abstinence movement, said Amy Stephens, a public policy representative for Focus on the Family in Colorado Springs, Colorado.

In 1992, she estimated, only about 10 groups promoted abstinence. Today (December 1997), there are more than 100.

Further highlighting the trend toward abstinence education is $50 million in federal funding annually for such curricula, which went into effect October 1, 1997, as part of the 1996 welfare reform legislation.

By funding abstinence, Congress has provided legitimacy to a different approach to sex education, Stephens said. Even people who once ridiculed Southern Baptists' True Love Waits campaign now admit abstinence belongs in mainstream education, she said.

However, the pro-abstinence camp has a long way to go, Stephens cautioned.

Many groups designing programs are trying to circumvent Congress' intent by mentioning abstinence but not presenting it as a clear-cut alternative, she said. The abuses are so flagrant they will be the subject of congressional hearings in 1998, she said.

"They have been wailing and shrieking about this money," Stephens said of groups like Planned Parenthood, the Sexuality Information and Education Council of the United States and others.

"Now, [premarital] sex advocates have stolen our language. They're talking about abstinence as one alternative, but giving it less emphasis than condoms. It's far different than those of us who would support waiting until marriage for sex."

That view is borne out by a recent letter from Debra Haffner, president of the council, to Minnesota Governor Arne Carlson. In it, she protested the policies of the newly formed National Coalition for Abstinence Education.

While the coalition favors restricted abstinence-only until marriage education, "there is wide-based support for broader educational approaches to educating young people about sexuality," Haffner wrote. "In (many) public opinion poll(s), Americans support the provision of sexuality education and HIV prevention."

Traditional Sexual Education Promotes Fallacies

Typically, sex education begins during middle school, although Stephens said it is entering elementary schools as children begin reaching puberty at a younger age.

One of the problems with traditional curriculum has been its "non-directive" philosophy, which presents all sexual choices as equal, she said.

Stephens said such an approach thrusts children into adult decision-making roles that are beyond their capacity. She compared it to asking them to walk through a field filled with land mines.

Although their thrust is to promote so-called safe sex, she added, supporters of this comprehensive health curriculum hide behind "pseudo science" and say they are simply providing information on HIV-AIDS, abortion and sexually transmitted diseases.

"Another fallacy taught is that our sexuality is on one continuum, that you can be straight today and gay tomorrow," Stephens said. "More kids than ever are questioning their sexuality because of the tremendous confusion thrown on them."

Young People Are Receptive to the Message

Despite the pro-abstinence movement's increasing numbers, Krauth said people who believe in waiting until marriage for sex need to concentrate on health issues. And they needn't be afraid of allowing the other side to speak, she said.

"A lot of Christians take this 'all or nothing' approach and get nowhere," said Krauth, a member of Mission Hills Church near Denver, Colorado. "We say let the condom people in and let us come in, and let the best man win.

"The research is on our side. I tell students I want to teach them how to have good sex, and that the best sex is in marriage. When I ask teens what they want to know, it's never about anatomy and physiology. Kids talk about caring, respect, dignity and boundaries."

WAIT Training is having a pronounced impact, she said, with about 30 percent of participants at one seminar saying they changed their mind about premarital sex.

Mullarkey said the new federal funding will result in more programs to help keep teens from damaging their lives.

"I can see it already in the hearts of these kids," she said. "They're overjoyed that somebody is saying they don't have to perform sexually. Some of the girls I see have shut down emotionally. They've been broken down because of early sexual involvement."

"Kids want to hear about abstinence," Stephens said. "It's adults who don't want to talk about it. If abstinence was promoted in this society, it's adults who would have to change their behavior."

Seeking Solutions: How Best to Teach Sexuality

Susan Okie

Susan Okie, a health writer for the *Washington Post,* addresses the issue of the most effective way to encourage sexual abstinence and prevent teen pregnancies. According to Okie, teens' decisions about whether and when to become sexually active hinge primarily on their relationship with their parents, their religious or moral values, and their socioeconomic status. Most educators and experts agree that open communication between parents and their children is key to helping teens make wise choices, she notes. Parents and schools both have important roles to play in sexuality education, she writes: Schools teach important information about sexuality, while parents impart personal and family values. Okie also reports that there is no conclusive proof that sex education programs encourage increased sexual activity among teens.

Spring sunshine lights up blank sheets of paper as six kids, aged 9 through 11, from Baltimore's Latrobe housing project grasp their pencils and get ready to draw their futures.

In a moment, the pencils begin to fly.

"I want to be a famous book writer for children's books," says Jasmine Bell.

"I want to be a lawyer," says Thion Grant.

"I want to go out in space. Then I want to get married," says Christopher Jones.

University of Maryland health educators Yvonne Summers, George Cornick and Jennifer Galbraith listen, smile and applaud those dreams. Then they shuffle a pack of cards and deal out some alternative fortunes.

"These are called adjustments to your future," they tell the children. "These are things that could go wrong and you have to figure out what you're going to do."

One card says, "You have tested positive for HIV." Another reads, "You got a girl pregnant."

Excerpted from Susan Okie, "Beyond the Birds and the Bees: Teaching Children to Make Responsible Decisions About Sex," *The Washington Post*, May 26, 1998. Copyright © 1998 *The Washington Post*. Reprinted with permission.

The kids' faces fall as they consider how such events might hobble their progress toward their goals. They discuss what they can do to keep them from happening.

"Use a condom," says Christopher. "Take those birthday pills."

"Don't have sex," suggest two other boys.

Cornick seizes on that response. "Don't have sex, that's correct," he says. "It looks like having sex when you're a teenager, or when you're too young, sets you up for a lot of trouble in the future."

Abstinence Versus Safe Sex

Don't have sex. Use a condom. Ever since the nation began to grapple with the AIDS epidemic in the mid-1980s, the issue of sex education for children and teens has acquired a life-and-death urgency. Multiple polls indicate that most Americans want schools to teach their kids what they need to know to avoid pregnancy and prevent sexually transmitted infections. At the same time, many adults worry about how best to transmit their own values to their children. The generation that once cautioned "Don't trust anyone over 30" are now parents themselves, and many are finding it as difficult as their own parents did to talk to their kids about sex, love and relationships.

"We had this cry from parents," said Bonita F. Stanton, a University of Maryland pediatrician who did community surveys in Baltimore before designing Focus on Kids, the program now underway at the Latrobe housing project and other sites. "They thought they were being inadequate, but they had no idea how to talk and what kinds of rules they should set."

The national debate over what children should be taught in sex education courses has been boiled down, in media reports and in many people's minds, to "abstinence versus condoms."

Many educators say the fight over abstinence versus condoms vastly oversimplifies the issue of how to provide children with truly comprehensive sexuality education. They argue that as children grow up, they need to be part of broad, age-appropriate discussions about gender roles, sexuality, communication and values that involve parents, schools, churches, the media and other sectors of society.

"Kids today learn about sex from here, there and everywhere," said Deborah M. Roffman, who has worked as a sexuality educator in Maryland for 27 years. "Openness in the news media about sexual topics is a real boon to our kids. They have a different baseline."

But that new societal openness doesn't necessarily mean that most children are getting what they need to become sexually responsible adults. Studies have shown that, while information is important, the quality of parent-child relationships, religious or moral values, socioeconomic status and family stability are critical determinants of children's decisions about whether and when to become sexually active.

Roffman and other educators said parents frequently overestimate how much their children learn about sexuality in school and how effective a sex education course, by itself, is likely to be in influencing their future behavior.

"Only 5 percent of young people receive anything like a comprehensive sexuality education program," said Debra W. Haffner, president of the Sexuality Information and Education Council of the United States (SIECUS).

SIECUS lists 36 topics that it considers part of such a comprehensive program. About 93 percent of U.S. high schools offer sexuality programs with information about the human immunodeficiency virus that causes AIDS, and the majority include information about puberty, abstinence, contraception, pregnancy and sexually transmitted diseases (especially AIDS). However, many programs tend to avoid certain other topics—particularly masturbation, abortion and homosexuality—which SIECUS recommends be covered.

Haffner said when she teaches eighth-graders about sexuality at her church's Sunday school, parents sometimes say to her, "Thank you for what you're giving my child for life." She said she tells them, "You can't do these programs as an immunization. I can give them what they need in the eighth grade. I can't prepare them to be 16 and in love—or 40 and in a 20-year-old marriage."

The Effects of Programs Vary

Yet studies suggest that some sexuality education programs can influence adolescents' behavior. During the 1990s, largely because of the AIDS epidemic, scientists have begun a concerted effort to evaluate how different types of educational programs affect children's actions—for example, whether kids who participate are less likely to have sex or more likely to use condoms. Such studies were partly prompted by the fear that providing information about condoms and birth control might actually increase sexual activity, especially among teenagers.

A wealth of studies now indicate that fear is unfounded. "The overwhelming weight of evidence indicates that sex education programs do not hasten the onset of sexual debut," says Brian L. Wilcox, a professor of psychology at the University of Nebraska–Lincoln who has reviewed the research. Nor do such programs increase the frequency of intercourse, the number of partners, teen pregnancy rates or the incidence of sexually transmitted diseases.

Indeed, recent statistics suggest that many teenagers are heeding messages about abstinence, birth control and condoms. The proportion of 15-to-19-year-old girls who are sexually active fell from 53 percent in 1988 to 50 percent in 1995. For boys in the same age group, the proportion fell from 60 percent to 56 percent. The percentage of 15-to-19-year-olds who reported using condoms the first time they had sex tripled between 1975 and 1995 (from 18 percent to 54 percent). The teen pregnancy rate has dropped in the past two decades, from 247 pregnancies per 1,000 sexually active teens in 1974 to 210 in 1994.

Just how much sex education programs may be contributing to these favorable trends isn't clear. Five educational programs, the newest of which is the University of Maryland's Focus on Kids, have been identified by the federal Centers for Disease Control and Prevention (CDC) as effective in HIV prevention because they have been shown to delay sexual initiation or increase condom use, based on the findings of well-designed scientific studies published in peer-reviewed journals. However, even these programs seem to have only "modest effects" on behavior, Wilcox said.

"They work with some teens but not all teens," he said. "Almost none has been replicated in different sites. They don't necessarily translate to different cultures and geographic contexts."

Scrutinizing a Program's Effectiveness

A teenager's decision about whether to have sex—and whether to use condoms or birth control—depends not just on what that child knows but also on a host of other factors, including self-esteem, communication and refusal skills, family and cultural attitudes about sex and childbearing, and access to contraception. Most sexuality education programs address only part of that mix.

"We have no Cadillac programs out there," said Wilcox. "We have a few Hondas. But mainly what we've got out there are Yugos, and the Yugos don't work well."

Federal lawmakers recently addressed the situation. In 1996, as part of the welfare reform law, Congress appropriated $50 million annually for five years that states could use to fund sex education programs that teach "abstinence only" until marriage. Funding began in 1998, and all states have applied for and accepted the federal money. It can't be used for programs that also discuss birth control and ways that sexually active teenagers can avoid sexually transmitted diseases. Despite this federal funding, few of the programs focusing on "abstinence only" have undergone careful scientific scrutiny to determine whether they're effective, Wilcox said.

In May 1998, for the first time, researchers reported a significant, although short-lived, effect on adolescent sexual behavior from an abstinence-only program evaluated according to a strict research design known as a randomized controlled trial. The study by Princeton psychology professor John B. Jemmott and two colleagues is one of the few that have tested such a program in this type of trial, which scientists consider the most bias-free method for comparing different treatments or interventions.

In the study, published in the May 19, 1998, *Journal of the American Medical Association,* 659 African American students from three Philadelphia middle schools were randomly assigned to one of three programs:

one that focused on abstinence, one that focused on "safer" sex and condoms, and one (the "control" group) that discussed health promotion without focusing on sexual behavior. Each program contained eight one-hour classes and took place on two consecutive Saturdays.

More Work Is Needed

When participants were surveyed three months after the programs ended, those in the abstinence program were significantly less likely than those in the control group to report having had sexual intercourse. But that difference had disappeared when participants were surveyed again six months and 12 months after completing the program.

In contrast, the safer-sex group reported more frequent condom use than did the control group when surveyed at three, six and 12 months.

Jemmott said it may simply be more difficult to persuade adolescents to be sexually abstinent than to use condoms. "One possibility is that there's more external pressure to have sex than there is external pressure not to use condoms," he said.

Wilcox said one of the largest scientific tests of an abstinence-only program was a California study, published in 1997, of a curriculum called Postponing Sexual Involvement (PSI), a five-session program for seventh- and eighth-graders. In that study, 10,600 students were randomly assigned to receive either their regular health education classes or to receive the regular classes plus PSI. Study participants were surveyed three months and 17 months after the program ended. Children who had participated in PSI were just as likely as those who had not to have become sexually active, to have become pregnant or to have gotten a sexually transmitted disease.

Jemmott said researchers have much to learn about how to make abstinence-only programs effective. "I would say there's been a lot more research on safer-sex interventions than on abstinence interventions," he said. "There needs to be more work in developing abstinence interventions so that we can learn how to sustain the effects."

The Need for a Clear Message

Douglas Kirby, a senior research scientist at California's ETR Associates and an expert on sex education curricula, noted that the more elaborate and comprehensive programs advocated by SIECUS haven't been thoroughly evaluated either. The few studies of such programs in the early 1980s suggested they increased teenagers' knowledge but didn't appear to reduce sexual activity. However, educators have learned a considerable amount since then about what components make a program likely to work. "Values neutral" programs that leave it up to kids to figure out what's best for themselves have not been found as effective in changing behavior as programs that take a clear position.

Research shows that the most effective programs share several key characteristics. For instance, Kirby said, all five programs that have been found by the Centers for Disease Control (CDC) to change kids' behavior focus clearly on reducing one or more behaviors that can lead to pregnancy or HIV infection. To get their point across, they incorporate a variety of teaching methods and materials, appropriate to the participants' age, culture and sexual experience. They also are based on recognized theories of behavior change that have been found effective in other settings.

They provide accurate information about the risks of unprotected sex and how to avoid those risks. They address social pressures that adolescents often face in relation to sex. They provide practice in communication and refusal skills, and take enough time to allow participants to complete the activities. And they are taught by trained teachers or peers who believe in the program.

"They give a clear message," said Kirby. "One may be, wait till you're older to have sex. Another may be, always use condoms when you have sex. Those are clear messages for different target groups. Every activity is designed to reinforce that message."

For example, during a single classroom session at the Latrobe housing project, kids first discussed their goals and how pregnancy, HIV infection or drug abuse might affect them. Then they talked about the steps they'd go through when making a tough decision and where they could turn for help.

They did a role-playing exercise in which they practiced asking a teacher for an appointment to talk about a problem. They made lists of places where they could seek information: a dictionary, a library, a hospital, a telephone book. Each then used the telephone to call an AIDS hot line and ask how the disease is transmitted. They played a game called "Human Knot," in which they linked hands, tangled themselves up, and had to disentangle each other by working together, without letting go.

Each part of the session provided not only information, but practice in communicating and coping.

"Sometimes, kids don't seem like they're listening, but if you put information in their heads . . . somewhere, down the line, you'll connect," said Cornick, who has worked with the Focus on Kids program for about two years.

Reducing Risky Behavior

Stanton, the University of Maryland pediatrician, designed Focus on Kids for African American children between the ages of 9 and 15 after community surveys in inner-city Baltimore showed that 40 percent of kids in that age group were sexually experienced. Parents identified their adolescents' risk of HIV infection as a major concern.

"Here, the initial sexual involvement is intercourse," Stanton said. "There isn't the period of a couple of years of light petting [followed by] heavy petting" first. The program seeks to get kids to postpone having intercourse until they are more mature and better able to plan and make decisions. "The older we can get kids before they engage in sex," the better, Stanton said.

Two other programs found effective by the CDC, "Be Proud! Be Responsible!" and "Becoming a Responsible Teen," were also developed to target African American youth. Two additional programs, "Reducing the Risk" and "Get Real About AIDS," were developed and tested in ethnically mixed populations in high schools in California and Colorado.

The CDC's Division of Adolescent and School Health identifies and helps disseminate effective curricula for reducing risky sexual behavior among adolescents as part of its Research to Classroom project, said Janet Collins, the division's branch chief. The idea is to find innovative, broadly applicable curricula that an average teacher can use and make them readily available to everyone.

"We package them, we train [teachers], we make them visible," Collins said. But it's up to local school districts to decide what kind of programs to adopt.

Shared Responsibilities

In the Washington area, policies on sexuality education in schools vary among local jurisdictions. But whatever the policy on the books, teachers have to be comfortable discussing sexuality for a program to be effective, said Barbara K. Huberman, director of training and sex education for Advocates for Youth, a Washington-based nonprofit organization. That usually requires training.

"You can have the most fabulous curriculum in the world," she said. "It will go into the drawer because that particular teacher is fearful, concerned about parental reaction or not comfortable dealing with these issues."

Roffman, the Baltimore sexuality educator, said parents and schools both have vital roles to play in teaching children about sexuality. "Parents have teachable moments that are crucially important, that come up as often as you look for them," she said. "As a child's parent, I am the only person who can tell my child what I think and value."

Schools, on the other hand, have methodology. "They have trained teachers, curricula, resources . . . and groups of peers who can be utilized, in the safety of a well-run sexuality course, to tell the truth to one another, to support one another," Roffman said.

At a recent session of Roffman's seventh-grade human sexuality course at the Park School, a private school in the Baltimore suburb of Brooklandville, that kind of communication was evident. Kids were asked to pair off and take turns telling each other (or a reporter who participated in the class) what they thought about issues like homosexuality, gender stereotypes and dating.

They had plenty to say. Catherine Rosen and Alina Odnopozova said they thought homosexuality was "totally normal" for some people. Josh Lauren said he found it easy to talk about sex with his dad. Michael Schaffer said he didn't like the ways people stereotype girls and boys, because "they fit for some people but not for everybody."

Roffman believes learning to communicate is at the core of becoming comfortable with sexuality throughout life. She said students in her high school classes are required to read two newspapers a day and discuss "all the sex articles" except the ones dealing with crimes and scandals. In the last few months they've talked about Viagra, the Iowa septuplets and the Supreme Court decision on a same-sex sexual harassment case.

"I have a rather simple philosophy," she said. "Those things you communicate well about, you handle well.". . .

Parental Supervision and Strong Values

When it comes to teenagers and sex, good parenting makes a big difference. For all the debate over sex education in schools, the evidence so far suggests that parents play a stronger role than school-based educational programs in encouraging sexual abstinence and preventing teen pregnancies.

Studies show that close parent-child relationships, close parental supervision and strong religious or moral values all reduce the chances that a teenager will have sex or become pregnant.

But many parents find it hard to talk to their kids about sex. Some worry that if they urge their adolescent not to have intercourse, yet also bring up condoms and contraception, they'll be sending a mixed message.

"It's hard for parents to tread the line of, 'When am I pushing sex?'" said Stanton. "It's a tough one."

The best way to make parent-child discussions about sex comfortable is not to treat the topic as unusual, said Kirby. Age-appropriate conversations about sex, love and relationships should start in childhood and continue throughout adolescence.

"You don't have a single conversation but multiple conversations," Kirby said. "Sex should be like lots of other topics—you discuss it for 20 seconds, then move on. You don't wait for kids to ask you questions, because they will get the message that this is something you don't talk about."

Haffner agreed with that approach. "If you want to talk to your teenager, you'd better be talking to your 4-year-old," she said. "For some kids, you will wait your whole life for them to ask a question. We don't wait for our children to ask to teach them how to cross the street."

Parents should listen to their child, but not hesitate to express their own values, Kirby suggests. "It's a good idea for parents to express their values about when and under what conditions young people should engage in sex—and to express their views about contraception," he said.

Parents Do Know More

One easy way to initiate a conversation about love, sex and values is to discuss the characters in a movie or television show. Haffner allows her 12-year-old daughter to watch the evening soap opera *Dawson's Creek,* but only if Haffner watches it with her. After each episode, they discuss the characters' relationships and behavior. She said her daughter doesn't usually find much to emulate.

Haffner said fear of giving mixed messages shouldn't deter parents. "We give mixed messages all the time," she said. For example, parents often tell their teenagers they shouldn't drink, but also warn them that if they do drink, not to drive.

"It's important to communicate your family's values about sex to your children," Haffner said. "The next part of the message is, 'If you are starting to think about having intercourse, I hope you will come and talk to me.'"

The third part should be, "It is critical that if you have intercourse, that you protect yourself by using contraception and condoms," she added.

Many parents complain that teens think they know all about sex already. But that's not what teenagers think, a survey suggests. In a nationally representative survey conducted in April 1998 for the National Campaign to Prevent Teen Pregnancy, only 6 percent of adolescents aged 12 to 17 thought they knew as much or more than their parents about sex and relationships. Topics that the teenagers wished their parents would talk more about included sexually transmitted diseases and birth control, how to manage dating and relationships, and knowing how and when to say "no."

CHAPTER 5

RISKS AND CONSEQUENCES: TEEN PREGNANCY

Contemporary Issues
Companion

THE FACTS OF TEEN PREGNANCY: AN OVERVIEW

The Annie E. Casey Foundation

The selection that follows is taken from a special report issued in 1999 by the Annie E. Casey Foundation, a private charitable organization headquartered in Baltimore, Maryland. According to the foundation, even though the teen pregnancy rate decreased considerably in the 1990s, the United States still has the highest rate of any industrialized country in the world. The report highlights various factors that contribute to the prevalence of teen pregnancy and discusses common misconceptions about teen sexual behavior. Communities and families can help prevent teen pregnancy, the foundation suggests, by providing accurate and consistent information about how to reduce risk-taking behaviors and supporting advocacy campaigns to encourage responsible portrayals of sexuality in the mass media.

The care and protection of children is, first and foremost, a family concern. But when teenagers have babies, the consequences are felt throughout society. Children born to teenage parents are more likely to be of low birth-weight and to suffer from inadequate health care, more likely to leave high school without graduating, and more likely to be poor, thus perpetuating a cycle of unrealized potential.

Despite a 20-year low in the teen pregnancy rate and an impressive decline in the teen birth rate, the United States still has the highest teen pregnancy rate of any industrialized country. About 40 percent of American women become pregnant before the age of 20. The result is about 1 million pregnancies each year among women ages 15 to 19. About half of those pregnancies end in births, often to young women and men who lack the financial and emotional resources to care adequately for their children. And when parents are financially and emotionally unprepared, their children are more likely to be cared for either by other relatives, such as grandparents, or by taxpayers through public assistance.

Experts estimate that the combination of lost tax revenues and increased spending on public assistance, child health care, foster care,

Excerpted from The Annie E. Casey Foundation, "When Teens Have Sex: Issues and Trends: A Kids Count Special Report," January 20, 1999. Used with permission.

and the criminal justice system totals about $7 billion annually for births to teens. In *Kids Having Kids: A Robin Hood Foundation Special Report on the Costs of Adolescent Childbearing,* researchers note that during her first 13 years of parenthood, the average adolescent mother receives AFDC and food stamps valued at just over $1,400 annually.

Hopeful Signs of Change

Recent declines in the pregnancy and birth rates are encouraging. The rate of pregnancies has dropped from a peak of 117 for every 1,000 young women ages 15 to 19 in 1990, to 101 in 1995. That 14 percent drop brought the rate to its lowest level since 1975. Similarly, the teen birth rate has dropped from 62 for every 1,000 young women ages 15 to 19 in 1991, to 54 in 1996—a 12 percent decline. During that 5-year period, the National Center for Health Statistics reports that the actual *number* of births to teens dropped by 5 percent, but is still close to half a million each year.

Every state and the District of Columbia experienced some decline in their teen birth rate between 1991 and 1996, from a 6 percent drop in Arkansas to a 29 percent drop in Alaska. In addition, the teen birth rate decreased among all races. The steepest decline—21 percent—occurred among black teenagers, whose rate of births is now the lowest in 40 years. Another hopeful sign is that nationally, the birth rate among 15- to 17-year-olds declined faster than that for 18- and 19-year-olds.

What's behind the overall drop in these rates? Some might speculate that the reduction in the teen birth rate results from an increase in the abortion rate. But the teen abortion rate (number of abortions per 1,000 females ages 15 to 19) fell from 41 in 1990 to 30 in 1995.

Rather than trying to deal with a pregnancy after the fact, more teenagers seem to be trying to *prevent* pregnancies. Researchers cite two main reasons for the overall drop in both pregnancy and birth rates: Fewer teens are having sex, and among those who are, more are using contraceptives. In a special analysis of the falling pregnancy and birth rates, Patricia Donovan of the Alan Guttmacher Institute (AGI) noted that researchers attribute the recent trends in teen sexual activity and contraceptive use to a variety of factors:

- greater emphasis on delaying sexual activity;
- more responsible attitudes among teenagers about casual sex and out-of-wedlock childbearing;
- increased fear of sexually transmitted diseases, especially Acquired Immune Deficiency Syndrome;
- the growing popularity of long-lasting contraceptive methods, such as the implant (Norplant) and the injectable (Depo-Provera) options, and possibly more consistent or correct use of other contraceptive methods; and
- a stronger economy, with better job prospects for young people.

The Youth Risk Behavior Surveillance System, conducted under the auspices of the Centers for Disease Control and Prevention, confirms that fewer teens are having sex. In 1997, 48 percent of the nation's high school students reported ever having had sex, compared to 54 percent in 1990. The overall rate masks important differences among subgroups. In 1997, 44 percent of non-Hispanic whites, 52 percent of Hispanics, and 73 percent of non-Hispanic blacks reported ever having had sex. But only 35 percent of all respondents said that they had been sexually active in the previous 3 months.

Reported rates of sexual activity dropped more dramatically among male teens than among female teens. Between 1990 and 1997, the percent of females who reported ever having had sex remained at 48 percent, but the rate among young men dropped from 61 percent to 49 percent. The rate declined most steeply among non-Hispanic white males, dropping from 56 percent to 43 percent. Among non-Hispanic black males the rate went from 88 percent to 80 percent and among Hispanic males, from 63 percent to 58 percent.

Demographic Concerns

At best, the downward trends in teen sexual activity call for cautious optimism. No one can predict whether the rates will continue to go down or pop back up again. So, it would be a mistake to think, merely on the basis of these hopeful signs, that the problem of teen pregnancy is close to being solved.

For starters, the teen birth rate is higher than it was 10 years ago. It's also worth re-emphasizing that the U.S. rates are still the highest in the developed world. The next closest nation, the United Kingdom, has a teen birth rate that is only about half that of the United States. And the high rate of childbearing among American teens is widespread. The Alan Guttmacher Institute reports that in 26 states and the District of Columbia, at least 1 out of every 10 teen females ages 15 to 19 became pregnant in 1992 (the latest year for which these figures are available). In every state, the pregnancy rate was higher than that of the United Kingdom. Equally troublesome is the fact that nationally, 22 percent of births were to teens ages 15 to 19 who already had a child.

Demographic trends confirm that the recent good news may be short-lived. As the children of the "baby boomlet" swell the ranks of American teenagers over the next few years, the absolute number of babies born to teenagers is likely to increase even if the birth rate remains constant. In fact, using the 1996 rate to project the number of births to women ages 15 to 19 in the year 2005 suggests a 14 percent increase in the number of babies born to teen mothers.

The majority of those births are likely to be out of wedlock, as were 76 percent of births to women ages 15 to 19 throughout the United States in 1996. Among the states, the percent of births that occurred to unmarried teens ranged from 58 percent in Utah to 92 percent in Rhode Island and 97 percent in the District of Columbia in 1996. According to the National Campaign to Prevent Teen Pregnancy, a private, non-partisan effort launched in 1996, the vast majority of unmarried teen mothers choose to keep their children rather than put them up for adoption.

Today's teen parents face very different circumstances than their counterparts of 30 years ago. During the 1960s, more than two-thirds of births to 15- to 19-year-olds occurred within marriage, even when conception occurred beforehand. At that time, marriage was viewed as an ultimate life goal, offering the financial and social stability that was considered essential for having and raising children. By the late 1980s, however, less than 40 percent of 15- to 19-year-olds who gave birth were married.

Among teen mothers in 1996, AGI reports that 84 percent of 15- to 17-year-olds and 71 percent of 18- to 19-year-olds were unmarried. Even though the stigma of out-of-wedlock births has lessened, "children growing up in single-parent households typically do not have the same economic or human resources available as those growing up in two-parent families," as noted in the Annie E. Casey Foundation's *1998 KIDS COUNT Data Book*.

Family structure is not the only factor that determines whether a child will succeed, but it has a definite impact, as sociologists Sara McLanahan and Gary Sandefur argue in their book, *Growing Up With a Single Parent*. They examined a decade's worth of data and found, "Compared with teenagers of similar background who grow up with both parents at home, adolescents who have lived apart from one of their parents during some period of childhood are twice as likely to drop out of high school, twice as likely to have a child before age twenty, and one and a half times as likely to be idle"—out of school and out of work—in their teens and early twenties."

The Human and Social Costs

The rates and numbers of teen pregnancies and births in the United States are cause for alarm, even with the recent dips. But it is the human and social costs of teen pregnancy and parenting that are most compelling. Premature parenthood is more than a 9-month interruption in a youth's life. Rather, it can further complicate a life that is already deficient in promise, hope, and dreams for the future.

A young woman who has a child before graduating from high school is less likely to complete school than a young woman who does not have a child. About 64 percent of teen mothers graduated from high school or earned a GED within 2 years after they would have graduated, compared with about 94 percent of teenage women who did not give birth. The failure to go further in school can limit the mother's employment options and increase the likelihood that she and her family will be poor. And the roughly one-fifth of adolescent moms who have more than one child are even more economically vulnerable. They might further delay finishing high school, putting them at greater risk of being slotted into low-wage jobs or of facing prolonged unemployment, poverty, and welfare.

For many teens, those risks are already high, and childbirth merely propels them further along a well-traveled path. That's because teens who give birth are more likely to come from disadvantaged family situations in which their life chances are already limited. While teen pregnancy touches all levels of our society, teens who give birth are more likely to come from economically disadvantaged families and communities, to be poor academic achievers with low aspirations, and to be coping with substance abuse and behavioral problems. Teen moms are also more likely to have mothers who completed fewer years of schooling and to have mothers or older sisters who also gave birth as adolescents.

Nearly 80 percent of teen mothers eventually go on welfare. According to Child Trends, more than 75 percent of all unmarried teen mothers went on welfare within 5 years of the birth of their first child. In fact, some 55 percent of all mothers on welfare were teenagers at the time their first child was born.

The consequences of early parenthood for teen fathers are generally not as severe as those for teen mothers, even though teen fathers are more likely to engage in delinquent behaviors and to use alcohol routinely, deal drugs, or quit school. Among married men studied by researchers in *Kids Having Kids,* those who were teen fathers had the least schooling. Also, researchers calculated that the fathers of children born to teen mothers earned an estimated average of $3,400 less a year than the fathers of children born to mothers who were 20 or 21, over the 18 years following the birth of their first child.

Consequences for Children

For many of the children of teen parents, the future is compromised even before they are born. Nationally, 10 percent of teens ages 15 to 19 who gave birth in 1996 received inadequate prenatal care. And, in Arizona, New Mexico, New Jersey, and the District of Columbia, more than 14 percent of teens did not receive adequate prenatal care. That undoubtedly helps to explain why babies born to teen mothers are about one-third more likely to be of low birth-weight (less than 5.5 pounds) than babies born to older women. Once born, the children of teen mothers face additional health risks. The infant mortality rate (deaths to children under age 1 per 1,000 live births) for children born to women under age 20 is about 50 percent higher than the rate for those born to women who are older than 20. The rate for children born to black or Native-American teen mothers is nearly twice that for children born to women who are older than 20. In addition, a recent study by the National Institute of Child Health and Human Development found that babies born to teen moms are at higher risk of abuse and neglect, including death.

Given the diminished economic prospects that many teen mothers experience, we should not be surprised that children born to unmarried women who are under the age of 20 and who have not completed high school are *10 times* more likely to be poor than children born to married women who are 20 or older and have a high school diploma. In 1996, the poverty rate for all children born to teen mothers was 42 percent, twice the overall rate for children. But income is not the only problem. Studies show that teen parents are generally less able to give their children the kind of solid foundation, including proper nutrition, health care, cognitive and social stimulation, and old-fashioned nurturing—in short, the things *all* kids need—to get off to a good start. . . .

Taken as a whole, society has to view the dangerous consequences of teenage sexual activity as an ongoing challenge. We should want to protect our teenagers from the risk of premature parenthood, and we should want to protect the children they would struggle to raise. If we are serious about breaking the cycles of poverty and underachievement that, too often, result from kids having kids, then we must not be satisfied with the recent downward trends, and we must expand our efforts to help those teens who are at greatest risk. Rather than becoming complacent because of the recent downturn, we must be more aggressive in implementing the positive lessons that contributed to it and redouble our efforts to cut the teen birth rate even more significantly. The National Campaign to Prevent Teen Pregnancy suggests a sensible goal of reducing the teen pregnancy rate by one-third between 1995 and the year 2005.

Preventing Teen Pregnancy

To accomplish this ambitious, but feasible, goal will require an unwavering commitment and aggressive action by both communities and families. It must be recognized that there is no magic solution to reducing teen pregnancy and childbearing rates, nor will a single intervention work for all teens. Because the decline from 1990 to 1996 is attributable to many factors, it is essential to continue and expand a range of programs that embrace many strategies. Experts agree that holistic, comprehensive, and flexible approaches are needed.

Communities and families need to provide accurate and consistent information about how to reduce risk-taking behaviors, such as unprotected sexual activity.

At a minimum, teens should be given basic information—about abstinence; about contraceptives, condoms, and other options for protection; and about their reproductive health. We need to talk to them more openly about the consequences of having a child and, certainly, about the consequences of having more than one child, before the age of 20. We need to more actively present to disadvantaged teens, in particular, a broader vision of their life possibilities. And we need to provide them with more targeted academic and job opportunities. An estimated 85 percent of teen pregnancies are unintentional. But, too many teenagers become parents either because they cannot envision another positive future direction to their lives, or because they lack concrete educational or employment goals and opportunities that would convince them to delay parenthood.

Teens also need access to specific information about how their bodies work and how to keep their bodies safe and healthy. Adults should recognize that young people need accurate, age-appropriate information about sexual behavior and its consequences. Whether or not they choose to have sex, teens need to develop skills in communication and sexual decision making so that sex does not just "happen."

Much relevant information about sexual behavior and its consequences can be conveyed through sex education classes, and a Harris Poll in 1988 found that 85 percent of adults support required sex education programs in schools. Yet a 50-state survey a decade later by Child Trends found that 19 states have an official policy requiring or encouraging pregnancy prevention programs in the public schools. In contrast, states have been much more aggressive in educating students about sexually transmitted diseases (STDs). All but 8 states have an official policy regarding HIV/AIDS education in their public schools. Despite that emphasis by states, many teens continue to take risks. Less than half of sexually experienced teen boys and only 38 percent of teen girls say they have used birth control every time they have had intercourse.

Presenting Clear Messages

Communities and families need to encourage more frequent and less ambiguous communication from adults, especially parents, on the issue of teenage sexual activity.

Today's adolescents are bombarded with a constant barrage of sexual images in popular culture, from advertisements to movies to song lyrics. Sex sells. But the sales pitch is often one-dimensional, ignoring the importance of values, emotional involvement, or the possibility of unintended consequences like pregnancy or disease.

Given these mixed messages about sex, and the fact that a large proportion of teens learn about sex from their friends, it is especially important for adults, particularly parents, to get past their own discomfort and have frank and open discussions with teens. In addition to basic information about sex, open communication can lead teenagers to seek the health counseling and services that they need.

Programs like the Casey Foundation's Plain Talk Initiative recognize the importance of reproductive health information and supports for teens—and the important role that adults play in providing them. Plain Talk has operated in five cities—San Diego, Hartford, Atlanta, New Orleans, and Seattle. It focuses on adults in the community, including parents and other relatives, teachers, neighbors, clinic service providers, ministers, and others, who interact with teens who may already be sexually active. The program seeks to create a community-wide consensus among parents and other adults to protect these youths from unintended pregnancies and disease. It also helps adults communicate more effectively with teens about responsible sexual decision making and behavior. And it helps mobilize adults to ensure that teens have access to good-quality, age-appropriate, and conveniently available reproductive health care, including contraceptives.

Community Reinforcements

Communities and families need to develop comprehensive, community-wide plans of action for adolescent pregnancy prevention, including adolescent reproductive health services, sexuality education, and programs to encourage young people to delay childbearing.

Adolescent reproductive health is not just about young women. Nor is it just about birth control pills. It encompasses an array of services, including comprehensive sex education; health promotion; and prevention of pregnancy, STDs, and HIV/AIDS. The challenge is to make clinical services available to teens in ways that increase their motivation and capacity to protect themselves.

Research, experience, and common sense confirm that, ideally, adolescent reproductive health services should include a site that is convenient to teens, such as a school or a mall; services for males as well as females; services that are provided during non-school hours, such as late afternoons, evenings, and weekends; non-medical services, such as peer education and mental health counseling; staff specifically selected and trained to work with adolescents; appropriate involvement of family members and significant others; confidentiality of patient information; and low-cost or free services. . . .

We must also recognize that contraception works for sexually active adolescents and that the recent drop in teen pregnancies and births is due, in part, to more consistent use of contraceptives by sexually active teens. Family planning is an important component of adolescent reproductive health. The Alan Guttmacher Institute estimates that as a result of publicly funded family planning programs, including clinics and family planning services, about 386,000 unintended pregnancies among females ages 15 to 19 are prevented each year. Beyond access to quality reproductive health services, all young people need comprehensive sexuality education to prepare them for healthy adult relationships. Effective programs give information about abstinence, healthy relationships, *and* contraception. They also help young people explore attitudes, feelings, and values about human development, dating, gender roles, sexual behavior, and healthy sexual decision making. They are most effective when they are culturally specific and focus on building skills, including the ability to say "no."

One model is Girls, Incorporated's Preventing Adolescent Pregnancy program. Girls, Inc. is a national youth organization, and their program provides females, ages 9 to 18, with the information, skills, and motivation-building activities they need to avoid early pregnancy and to plan full, satisfying lives. The program has four components targeting specific age groups. Starting with the youngest participants, the program focuses on building positive parent/daughter communication about sexuality and values (ages 9 to 11), emphasizing how to recognize and resist pressure to become sexually active (ages 12 to 14), setting life goals that include using abstinence or contraception to avoid pregnancy (ages 15 to 18), and linking participants with community-based health services, including access to contraception (ages 12 to 18).

Another program that is widely used in communities across the country was developed for seventh and eighth graders by the Emory University School of Medicine and the Grady Memorial Hospital Teen Services Program in Atlanta, Georgia. One component of the program, called Postponing Sexual Involvement, employs older teens to teach younger people how to resist social and peer pressure to become sexually active. A second component, Respecting Your Future, enlists nurses and counselors to provide basic information about teen sexuality, including methods of protection against pregnancy and STDs. Overall, the program promotes more open dialogue about reproductive health between parents and their children, from the preteen years through adolescence.

Motivational Opportunities

Communities and families need to give young people a real vision of a positive future by investing time and resources to help them acquire good decision-making, communication, and work skills that prepare them for the adult world.

It is essential to help those teens at highest risk of pregnancy learn about educational and economic opportunities and about how to cope with the many social and psychological factors associated with risky sexual behavior. A number of approaches are needed to reach these teens, including counseling for and treating sexual abuse, drug and alcohol use, and/or family distress; mentoring by an adult with whom a close relationship can be developed; providing educational opportunities, including tutoring and access to higher education; offering recreational activities, such as sports, drama, and social clubs; developing vocational and job skills and helping with job placement; and providing community service opportunities.

Many of these approaches are encompassed in the Pregnancy Prevention Program of the Children's Aid Society in New York. This is a long-term, holistic, multidimensional adolescent sexuality and pregnancy prevention program for youths, parents, and adults. Its many components include job clubs and career awareness; family life and sex education; medical and dental services; mental health services; education and tutoring; guaranteed college admission upon completion of high school in some locations; lifetime individual sports; and self-expression through the arts. A 1995 study of the program found that it had positive effects on participants—delaying initiation of sex, increasing use of condoms among those who were having sex, and decreasing pregnancy rates.

Similarly, the Teen Outreach Program (TOP), currently managed by the Cornerstone Consulting Group, is being implemented in about 125 sites around the country in school-based and out-of-school youth programs aimed at 12- to 17-year-olds. TOP combines life skills and adolescent reproductive health education with youth involvement in community service. An educational component occurs in small groups with a facilitator who also serves as a mentor. Studies have shown that the program helps reduce pregnancy rates.

While evaluations lag behind promising practices, communities can find what works and then integrate the research and lessons learned from effective programs into local strategies and plans of action.

Improving Media Images

Communities and families should support advocacy campaigns to encourage responsible portrayals of sexuality in television, movies, and other mass media.

Campaigns that address teen sexuality can be direct or indirect. Plain Talk is one example of how caring adults take a direct approach in presenting clear, strong, and positive messages to teens. The Kaiser Family Foundation has successfully taken an indirect approach by persuading some television shows to include more realistic story lines that deal with adolescent reproductive health. Increased efforts to work with screenwriters, musicians, producers, advertisers, and other opinion molders to put different media images and messages before teenaged audiences should be pursued.

Parents can also use television and other mediums of popular culture, even controversial news events, to talk more, and more openly, with their children about sex and its consequences. In *Families Matter,* a publication issued by the National Campaign to Prevent Teen Pregnancy, Brent C. Miller found, "While parents cannot *determine* whether their children have sex, use contraception, or become pregnant, the quality of their relationships with their children can make a real difference."

The unacceptably high rates of teen childbearing can be reduced, as evidenced by the promising dip in recent years. However, much work remains to be done to ensure that the downward trend continues. Fortunately, more information is becoming available to help identify young male and female teens who are at risk for early parenthood. We also have better information to help us curb the spread of sexually transmitted diseases that threaten growing numbers of young Americans. And we know more about effective practices that have promising evaluation results for community-based programs that can be replicated throughout the nation.

Taking the measures that we have outlined—and reaping the benefits they can bring—is contingent upon recognizing that the physical development of teens is often out of sync with their emotional and cognitive development. More important, they are often exposed to inconsistent and confusing messages about sex and sexuality from parents, schools, communities, and the media. These realities are not going to disappear. But growing public recognition of the negative consequences of unprotected sex and the role of parents and communities in helping young people to acquire the skills to protect themselves gives us an opportunity to reinforce the hopeful trend that is reducing the incidence of children having children. We cannot fail to capitalize on this opportunity.

Myths and Facts

Opinion and myth abound regarding the cause and extent of teen pregnancy and births. The issues, fueled by media coverage and by personal experience and observation—and the emotional nature of the topic—are often clouded by erroneous assumptions. Over the past decade, however, careful studies have been able to examine and to measure more objectively adolescent sexuality in the United States. By asking teenagers more directly about their own views on sex, pregnancy, and childbearing—and by reassessing the male role in teen pregnancy prevention—many popular beliefs on the subject have been found to be unsupported by facts. Drawing on recent research, here are some common misperceptions and the facts that help correct them. . . .

Myth: Teenagers don't care about what parents think or say.

Fact: Young people rank parents as the *preferred* source of information about sex and health. They also rank parents as the most trusted source, and 1 out of 2 teenagers say that they trust their parents most for reliable and complete information about birth control. Only 1 in 10 say that they trust a friend most. When asked about the reasons why teenage girls have babies, about 3 out of 4 teenagers cited a lack of communication between a girl and her parents.

Myth: The high incidence of teen births is a new development in America.

Fact: The rate of teen births in the United States has been high for a long time. In the 1950s, the rate was as high as 90 births per 1,000 young women ages 15 to 19. By 1986, the rate had declined to 50, but by 1991, it had risen again to 62. What has changed is the proportion of births to *unmarried* teens. In 1960, only 15 percent of teen births were to unmarried teens, but in 1996, the figure was 76 percent.

Myth: The recent decline in the teen birth rate is due to an increase in abortions.

Fact: Along with pregnancy and birth rates, abortion rates also have declined. The teen abortion rate (number of abortions per 1,000 females ages 15 to 19) fell from 41 in 1990 to 30 in 1995. Of course, preventing pregnancies will reduce reliance on abortion to avoid unwanted births. . . .

Myth: Teen pregnancy is only a problem of minority populations.

Fact: Every year, 1 million young females in the United States get pregnant. Just over half of those pregnancies result in births; one-third result in abortions; and about one-sixth result in miscarriages. Consequently, the United States has the highest teen pregnancy, teen birth, and teen abortion rates of any industrialized nation. In 1997, about 45 percent of mothers ages 15 to 19 were white, 27 percent were black, 25 percent were Hispanic, and 3 percent were from other racial or ethnic groups. From 1991 to 1996, the teen birth rate for blacks fell more sharply than for whites or Hispanics and is currently the lowest ever recorded.

THE POLITICS OF TEEN PREGNANCY

Kristin Luker

In the following selection from her book *Dubious Conceptions: The Politics of Teenage Pregnancy*, Kristin Luker contends that teen pregnancy has become a political issue. Most conservatives, she writes, consider teen pregnancy the result of bad values and unwise choices; they view young unwed mothers as primarily being inner-city teens who expect to be supported by welfare. On the other hand, she maintains, most liberals believe the fundamental problem behind teenage pregnancy is poverty and call for training programs to help disadvantaged teenage mothers to become more productive, educated, and self-sufficient. In Luker's opinion, both sides have distorted views of the issue. She asserts that many poor teens make a conscious decision to have a baby, one of the few choices available to them that seems to hold the promise of a better life. Luker is a professor of sociology and law at the University of California at Berkeley.

In the 1970s advocates of a public policy aimed at curbing early childbearing promised a cure for many of America's social ills. They argued that everything from dropout rates to infant mortality to poverty could be reduced if teens just had fewer babies. Back then, reducing early pregnancy and childbearing had political appeal for both conservatives and liberals. Conservatives wanted teens to be less active sexually, to have fewer abortions, and to wind up less often as single mothers on Aid for Families with Dependent Children (AFDC). Liberals wished to help young women gain control over their reproductive and sexual destinies, thereby ensuring that untimely births would not limit young women's opportunities and chain them to a lifetime of poverty. In achieving these goals, liberals preferred to use a carrot; conservatives, a stick. By the 1970s traditional conservatives, who were worried primarily about the economic dimensions of early childbearing, had been joined by members of the New Right, who were concerned primarily about its moral implications. But in those days, the public did not yet perceive the issue as being an extremely urgent social problem.

Now, some two decades later, the debate over early childbearing has become more heated and widespread. As the economy has slowed and Americans have begun to have a harder time finding and keeping jobs, resentment against certain entitlements has escalated; unwed teenage mothers have been a target of particular scorn. The economy is showing even more of a tendency to bifurcate into an upper, affluent tier and a lower, poorer one—a situation in which workers with high-level skills are reaping more and more rewards. Middle-class people have developed ways of adapting to these pressures: they postpone childbearing until they have gotten enough education to compete for dwindling white-collar jobs, and they form two-earner households so that they can afford a home, live in a safe neighborhood, and send their children to good schools.

Teenagers who have babies don't conform with these middle-class assumptions and expectations. Looked at through middle-class eyes, such teens seem to be closing themselves off from the education that could make them self-supporting and take them off the public dole. They also appear to be limiting their ability to find a husband who could support them, thus making it likely that they will remain unwed and on welfare. As the average incomes of most Americans diminish in real value, the public becomes more restive about welfare and the taxes that support it. All women with dependent children who receive benefits are the targets of public anger these days, but young mothers, who account for a tiny portion (about 8 percent) of the women on welfare, provoke special rage. To Americans who are increasingly postponing marriage and childbearing and are limiting the number of children they have, "babies having babies" looks like a recipe for trouble. Worse yet, it's a trouble that young people seem to bring on themselves but that everyone else seems to have to pay for. Not surprisingly, the major political parties have tapped into the public's resentment and now devote special attention to pregnant teenagers.

For most conservatives, early childbearing, especially out of wedlock, is the result of bad values and unwise choices. They see young mothers as inner-city teens who lack stability and guidance, engage in irresponsible behavior, and then expect to be supported by the state. They believe that the welfare system offers what economists call "perverse" incentives—that its mere existence incites young women to get pregnant and live off its bounty. Their remedy: restrict access to welfare, particularly in the case of teenagers. . . . According to the conservative view, young unwed mothers are rational actors who pursue a course that they see as being in their self-interest; denying teenagers welfare and limiting benefits to older women will reduce the rate of out-of-wedlock births.

Despite a great deal of evidence to the contrary, many people still believe that welfare benefits cause early and out-of-wedlock childbearing. . . .

A Morally Complex Choice

But although incentives certainly affect behavior, they do so in a moral and social context that shapes how people interpret those incentives. For all women—rich and poor, teenage and older—decisions regarding childbearing and marriage have a great deal to do with feelings, values, beliefs, and commitments. They are rarely governed solely by the availability of a welfare check.

When speaking about their decision to have and raise a child, young mothers use terms that in other contexts would seem praiseworthy. They stress that they are attempting to take responsibility for their actions, sexual and otherwise. They have difficulty accepting abortion and adoption—the ways in which young women have traditionally hidden their shame from society—precisely because these alternatives do permit women to act as if nothing had happened. To be sure, the moral calculus here includes a measure of self-interest: for young women to whom few good things happen, childbearing offers at least the possibility of making a change in life. But the decision to bear and raise a child is not only a selfish one. Many young women describe how morally complex the choice is:

> Because his [the baby's] father, he didn't believe in abortion, he said I'm here, you're here, so why can't he come in as well? Don't kill the baby, he's going, we already made it. So we discussed that, too, before I got pregnant, if I got pregnant, that I should keep it because it ain't right to just throw away a life, so I said OK. (Lynn, teenager, black)

> I wasn't ready . . . and I thought I should wait a little longer and finish finding pleasure, but my mother didn't want that and she made sure I kept the baby. And afterwards I was, like, hey, why not? I started feeling the same, I wanted it, too. It wasn't just like I had it because she wanted me to and stuff. My mother said she wants all her grandchildren. (Liz, sixteen, black, Boston)

> You make your bed, you lie in it. (White teenager, living in the rural Northeast)

> If I'm responsible enough to be goin' out and doin' these things getting pregnant, then I should be responsible enough to handle what I got myself into. (Sally, seventeen, white, rural Northeast)

Seeing a Child as an Opportunity

A variety of incentives blend together here. Young African American women know that few families want to adopt a minority child. Some young white and black women, like some of their elders, have moral scruples about abortion; and they believe that raising a child gives a young woman an opportunity to be good at something even if she must make sacrifices. In a poor neighborhood squeezed by a declining economy, there are often few opportunities to be responsible. But motherhood provides that opportunity, as well as a spur for a young woman to try to make something of herself:

> I know I have to go to school because of the responsibility of the baby. It [having the baby] gave me a better outlook on life. I have to be concerned about the baby's future. (Black teenager, Los Angeles area)

> Mrs. J. talks about this all the time. She makes us responsible for everything. She says we have two lives to consider now, and she's right.

> I think it [having a baby] will press me on to do better and to do more, 'cause I want my child to have, you know, basically everything. And it will help me to do better in school and achieving the goals that I want to. I feel I can handle it. I feel that this baby will push me to strive for what I'm looking for, for a better life. I want my child to have a better life. I'm not sayin' my life is bad, I'm sayin' so it will have what it wants. I think that when you have somethin' right there before you, you have a real goal. You see, when I have that baby there, I say, you got to buckle down, you got to get good grades, you got to get the best.

In fact, some young women outright reject the notion that economic considerations should be the primary motive in the decision to have a child:

> I know it's hard to try and bring somebody into the world when you're not rich. But that's it, that's just it, everybody around is not rich and people who are rich are doin' worse by their kids than the people who don't have . . . It don't matter if you don't have the money or the know-how, 'cause stuff like that come . . . Experience, it come with havin' a baby. I know I will never have a lot of money, but what I do have will be for the baby.

Poverty Is the Problem

The moral reasoning that undergirds the decision to have and raise a child is of course shaped by the larger world, the "incentives" that conservatives like to talk about. But the most visible incentive—welfare—has been declining in real value at precisely the time that more teenagers are deciding not to marry, and birthrates among teens have been stable or declining for most of the past two decades. . . .

The problem that confronts poor young people in the 1990s is the dearth of real alternatives to welfare. In the 1950s and 1960s, a young man could support a family on a low-wage job. There are fewer such jobs now, and they pay less: a minimum-wage job no longer allows a man to support a family or a single mother to support a child, even if they work full time and year round. If a woman has to pay for child-care, she earns less working than she would get on welfare. This poses a dilemma for the American public: poor people can't earn enough to support a family, but no one wants to support them on welfare. One solution is the course advocated by policymakers in the nineteenth century: people who cannot afford to have children should simply stay childless. More humane, but ultimately deceptive, is the notion that poor teens should postpone their childbearing until they are emotionally and financially ready. People who identify early child-bearing as the core of the poverty problem believe that teenagers are only temporarily unfit for parenthood and that they will mature into it. Alas, many of these young people will never be ready, at least if we define "ready" as having enough money to support themselves and their children. Given the scarcity of decent jobs, a substantial minority of Americans simply cannot afford to have children without some form of social transfer. A child born to married parents who can fully support it is, like safe neighborhoods and good schools, becoming a luxury accessible only to the wealthy.

Liberal critics of early pregnancy have their own form of myopia about the problem. They realize that the fundamental problem is poverty, but they argue that society should make a greater investment in teenage mothers—that it should create training programs to increase the human capital that young mothers possess and hence increase their long-term self-sufficiency. From the liberal point of view, teenage mothers are disadvantaged people who would be much less likely to stay poor if they did a few simple things: finished their education, postponed childbearing, found a husband, and acquired marketable skills. Although this prescription sounds straightforward and com-monsensical, it ignores the fact that most young mothers inherit mul-tiple problems. They were born poor and grew up in poor neighbor-hoods. Their early lives were often scarred by violence and disorder, including sexual abuse. They attended rundown, underequipped schools in which teachers struggled to discipline and motivate the stu-dents, and they were typically not among the lucky and clever few who managed to obtain a little extra attention from their teachers, coaches, or adult neighbors. They were born into families that were at the end of the social and economic queue, and their life experiences rarely moved them any closer to the front. By having babies, such women are manifesting an almost poignant hope—the hope that a better future lies ahead, for their children if not for themselves.

Thus, training programs have very real limits. Even the good ones can only reshuffle people who are standing at the end of the line, not fundamentally transform the nature of the line. If young mothers acquire more training and skills, at best they simply displace others a step or two ahead of them. Most training programs for young women on welfare have a high rate of success, but this success is very specific: such programs raise the income of participants by amounts that exceed the cost of the program. Unfortunately, these women are so poor that this higher income typically raises their financial status only slightly—from desperately poor to miserably poor. If teenagers and their babies represented only poverty in its traditional form—if they were members of poor two-parent families or were worthy widows, as in earlier decades—the public might be more willing to spend resources to bring them and their children into the mainstream. But poverty today brings with it new family structures that many Americans find troubling.

Unease About New Family Structures

Poor people are more likely to become parents as teenagers than are affluent people, and they are also more likely to have babies out of wedlock. So when conservatives claim, despite all findings to the contrary, that welfare causes early and out-of-wedlock childbearing, they speak to a public worried about two different things—the cost of welfare and changing family structures—in a way that knits these two concerns together. Liberals have been slow to make this distinction: they constantly remind conservatives that AFDC accounts for only a small fraction of federal spending, especially when compared to other federal programs such as the military. They are correct on this point: even the cost of middle-class welfare programs (Social Security, Medicare, deductions for home-mortgage interest) dwarfs the amount spent on AFDC. Social Security in particular, because it is indexed to inflation, has become a significant income-transfer program for middle-class people: most individuals take out far more in benefits than either they or their employers made in contributions. But liberals have been slow to realize that the public is extremely uneasy about the way family structures have changed, and that this unease has settled on the heads of teenagers and women on welfare. Americans find welfare troubling when it seems to encourage early and out-of-wedlock childbearing, especially among the poor and minorities.

Since the signs of poverty and these new family structures have become more widespread simultaneously, conservatives make a seemingly logical argument when they relate the two. People who believe that welfare is wrong if it creates more single and teenage parents are drawing on a valid intuition: that the more adults there are who are committed to the well-being of a child, the better off that child is.

Likewise, they are almost certainly right to suspect that the ties uniting parents with children and husbands with wives have frayed in the last twenty years. They are also right to think that children benefit when their parents have more resources—emotional, spiritual, psychological, financial—to devote to them, and that such resources are becoming ever scarcer. They are wrong, however, in assuming that welfare has had much to do with these unfortunate social trends.

The troubles that teenage parents face today are the same ones that all Americans face: changes in the nature of marriage, in the relations between men and women, in the relations between parents and children. Everyone is having difficulty mustering the emotional, psychological, and financial resources that children need, and many people long for the days when life seemed easier. But Americans are wrong when they assume that teenage parents suffer disproportionately from these problems because they are young; rather, teenage parents are vulnerable parents because they are poor. Society runs the moral risk of scapegoating teenage mothers—symbolically punishing them for trying to solve the problems everyone faces and solve them with more limited resources than most Americans.

Does this mean that people should shrug their shoulders and say that early childbearing is just a fact of modern life? No. The increase in the number of teenage and unwed mothers is an indirect measure of the toll that a bifurcating economy is taking on Americans, especially women of poor and minority backgrounds. It would be better to see early childbearing as a symptom, like infant mortality—not a cause but a marker of events, an indicator of the extent to which many young people have been excluded from the American dream. It is distressing and alarming that early childbearing—like infant mortality—is more common among minorities, the poor, and those who have been failed by the nation's major institutions. In addition, the plight of teenage mothers reveals not only how hard it is to be poor in America, but the special pressures that confront young, poor women. One of the tragedies of early childbearing is that it is one of the few ways in which such women feel they can make a change in their lives, however illusory that change may prove to be. Having a baby can give a young woman permission to be assertive and motivated on her baby's behalf when she has trouble mustering these qualities for herself. For example, a woman disillusioned with education may decide to stay in high school because she doesn't want her baby to have a dropout for a mother. The fact that birthrates among teens have stayed at high levels indicates how discouraged and disadvantaged many young women are—that they have to take the extraordinary step of bearing a child in order to feel they have a meaningful role and mission in society and can make claims on themselves and others.

Having a baby is a lottery ticket for many teenagers: it brings with it at least the dream of something better, and if the dream fails, not much is lost. Some young women say it was the best thing they ever did. In a few cases it leads to marriage or a stable relationship; in many others it motivates a woman to push herself for her baby's sake; and in still other cases it enhances the woman's self-esteem, since it enables her to do something productive, something nurturing and socially responsible. Yet lotteries are by definition unpredictable. To the extent that babies can be ill or impaired, mothers can be unhelpful or unavailable, and boyfriends can be unreliable or punitive, childbearing can be just another risk gone wrong in a life that is filled with failures and losses. Although early childbearing rarely causes a young woman to be poor and discouraged, once she is responsible for a baby a woman may find that she has a harder time taking advantage of lucky breaks and fewer opportunities to make positive changes in her life. What should trouble us when we worry about teenage parents is the fact that poor and minority women feel they risk losing so little by having a child at an early age. American society places great value on individual success, and is remarkably stingy in its support of those who "fail." It is no accident that in the United States—where the penalties for failure are so severe—the birthrate among teenagers is higher than in any other industrialized nation, and 80 percent of babies born to teens are born to poor women. If young men and women felt they had an array of opportunities in life and still chose to become parents as teenagers, their decision would evoke comparatively little concern. But in fact early childbearing is a very constrained choice for poor people who have few other options; for them, being a teenage parent can be much more rewarding and much less costly than is generally supposed. If America cares about its young people, it must make them feel that they have a rich array of choices, so that having a baby is not the only or most attractive one on the horizon.

PARENTS CAN HELP PREVENT TEEN PREGNANCY

Sheri McGregor

Parents should not leave sex education to the schools, maintains journalist Sheri McGregor in the following selection. McGregor contends that the problem of teen pregnancy cuts across all racial, social, and economic lines. Nevertheless, she notes, most parents are unaware of their children's sexual activity and are shocked when their teenaged daughter becomes pregnant. Parents can take steps to prevent teen pregnancy, she writes, by talking candidly to their children about sex, preferably beginning before the child turns thirteen. However, even older teens—including those who are already sexually active—will benefit from conversations with parents about sex, McGregor avers. McGregor is a former columnist on parenting resources for *Real Woman Magazine*.

With AIDS bringing the safe sex hype to the media forefront, the problem of teen pregnancy gets second billing. But with more than half of kids in the U.S. engaging in sexual intercourse before the age of 18, the teen pregnancy epidemic is real.

Sadly, the United States boasts a rate of teen pregnancy more than twice as high as any other developed country. Here, an estimated 56 helpless babies are born to teen mothers *every hour*, and those numbers are growing.

The age of these young moms is shocking. Dana Serrano, Administrative Director at Alternatives Pregnancy Care Clinic in Escondido, California, says "Most of the pregnant girls in our Teen Life Program are aged 14 and 15." And one pediatrician I spoke with said it's commonplace for him to check a newborn in one exam room, then go up the hall to care for the other baby—its 13-year-old mother!

Why Are So Many Teens Getting Pregnant?

"The attitude that permeates our teenagers' lives is that having sex is just like eating a bowl of cereal," said one mother whose teen became pregnant at age 15. She and her husband were shocked by their

Reprinted from "Teen Pregnancy: Face the Facts Before You're Forced To," by Sheri McGregor, *Parenting Today's Teen*, www.parentingteens.com. Used with permission.

daughter's sexual activity. They're a nice middle class family who goes to church regularly.

"There were no glaring problems," the mother says of her daughter. "But when we began to look at everything influencing her life: MTV, the music she was listening to, and the places she was buying her clothes, we found that all those areas promoted a sexuality that surprised us, and that we'd been looking at it in a very benign way."

Should parents worry about the sexuality marketed to our kids and the peer pressure it results in? Some good advice comes from Michelle, a teen who became pregnant after a prom night party. She says, "The biggest influence on teens to have sex comes from their peers. Especially around the ninth grade when many kids think they have to lose their virginity to be 'cool.'"

When asked what parents might do to help combat the problem, Michelle offered, "Parents need to become more aware of what really goes on in their children's lives, and get more involved—even if that may mean their kids don't like them for a few years."

Michelle gives the scenario of a girl wanting to go to a party her parents don't feel comfortable letting her attend. When the daughter throws a fit, saying it isn't fair, even telling her parents that she hates them, they give in, either to please their daughter or to end the fighting.

Michelle, who believes a lot of problems might be solved if parents *didn't* give in, says, "Parents need to supervise everything their kids do, no matter how it affects their teen's feelings at the moment."

Who Is at Risk?

The problem of teen pregnancy has no social, economic or racial boundaries, yet, according to Heather Hunter, a counselor at the Life Choices Pregnancy Center in Poway, California, "Parents are always surprised." Hunter believes that in addition to other factors, a lack of supervision plays a large role in the prevalence of teen pregnancy. With single-parent and two-income households the norm, "Parents aren't always there to chaperone."

But it's not that simple. Michelle, a successful student who maintained a 3.5 GPA, comes from a two-parent family with a stay-at-home mom. She says she was well-supervised, and has ". . . always lived in a very nice area, and gone to good schools." Girls like Michelle aren't the exception.

Alternatives Director Serrano believes the catch phrase "Just Say No," proven effective in the drug and alcohol arena, should be applied to the issue of sex, too. She says, "With the media focusing on safe sex, kids have a false sense of security. They don't realize condoms have a 15 percent failure rate." In educating teens through her work at the Alternatives Clinic, Serrano found that 73 percent are surprised to learn that contraception isn't foolproof.

Prevention: What's Being Done?

In San Diego County, California, Debbie Bronstein has initiated and runs the nonprofit program, S.T.O.P. (Students Thinking Over Parenthood). With grant monies, Bronstein takes the nationally used newborn simulation doll, "Baby Think It Over," into schools free of charge. The crying doll, along with car seats, strollers and other equipment essentials Bronstein provides, gives junior high and high school students a sobering dose of parenting reality.

Although no feedback statistics on pregnancy rates for students who've participated in the San Diego program are yet available, according to students' comments taken before and after their simulation experience, the doll is making its mark.

Are school and community programs like this one enough?

Prevention Begins at Home

Mirroring what many teens report, Michelle says her parents never talked to her about sex, and that she wouldn't have been comfortable approaching them. But teen pregnancy professionals agree that discussion between parents and kids is essential.

Serrano cautions parents not to leave it to the schools to teach their kids about sex. She also advises parents to educate themselves first, so they can relay accurate facts, enabling their kids to make wise choices.

Even with education, many parents feel awkward. How do you initiate a conversation about sex?

According to "Not Me Not Now," a program created in Monroe County, New York, the direct approach is best. The program suggests beginning a serious discussion by sharing an experience from your own adolescence. You might relate what you first heard about sex from your friends, or how your school introduced the subject. Once you've broken the ice, tell your child directly that you think it's important the two of you talk about sex. Or, ask what he or she has heard, or wants to know.

And don't forget to listen! You may be surprised at your child's desire to talk with you. Give your son or daughter the information they want, as accurately as you can. If there's something you're not sure about, make a commitment to getting that information, and learning it together.

Experts say these initial conversations should come early, preferably before the age of 12. Even if you think your pre-teen is too young to be interested in sex, it's important to get the dialog going early. Kids under 12 are more easily influenced by their parents' feelings than when they're just one year older.

Tell your child what you expect. Share your moral beliefs and concerns, and do it now, while your viewpoints can make an impact. Hopefully, they'll still have those values in mind when faced with peer pressure and strong desires later.

What About Older Teens?

It's never too late. The cliché rings true here as well as anywhere. It may be more difficult to get conversations going with kids in the 13- to 15-year range when their peers and the media have more influence than parents, but continue to look for opportunities. Get to know your teen's friends. Watch television with your son or daughter, and force yourself to listen to their music. You might gain some insight into what they're thinking.

If you suspect your teen is having sex, don't delay in taking action. You may not be able to stop him or her, but you can caution against possible consequences. Call a center for help if you need it.

Most of all, be approachable. Let your teen know how much you care. Your love and supervision, tempered with realistic, direct discussion and education, really can make a difference in preventing teen pregnancy.

Teenage Parenting: A Personal Account

Julie Jeffrey

> In the selection that follows, school psychologist and About.com guide Julie Jeffrey gives an account of her interview with a pair of teen parents she calls Laura and Charlie. Seventeen years old and juniors in high school, Laura and Charlie decided to keep their baby but not get married. Laura and the baby live with Laura's parents. Although Charlie does not live there with them, he knows he always is welcome to visit—which he does regularly. Laura and Charlie acknowledge that their lives have become very different since the birth of their baby and admit that they do not know what the future will bring. But they agree that they love their son and, according to Jeffrey, they have found a way to cope with being teen parents.

As anyone who is a parent knows, there is no greater moment than the one where you hold your newborn baby for the first time. It seems like at that moment there is nothing in the world that can compare. For many parents, we bundle up our newborns, take them home and move on with life—and life becomes the richer for having added a child.

Ok . . . now add the fact that mom and dad are still in high school. It is spring and the prom is coming up, and so is "senior skip-day," and the once active social life you had as a high school student is now changed. Not necessarily for the worse, but different. You have decided to become a parent. Maybe you didn't mean for it to happen, but happen it did, and as a teen you have become a mom or a dad. What can be a normally joyous occasion has now become a very stressful event. The added responsibility of parenthood has been added to your life as a high school student or teenager, and life has been turned upside down.

Laura: A Teen Mom

"I love my baby very much. He is so special and everyone loves him just as much as I do," Laura states as she rocks her son in her arms. She is sitting in the living room of her parents' home holding her son

Reprinted, with permission, from "A Teen's Story," by Julie Jeffrey, About.com Guide to Single Parents, March 21, 2000. www.singleparents.about.com/library/weekly/aao21900c.htm.

close. He is just four months old. Laura is a 17-year-old high school junior with brown hair and big blue eyes.

"Yeah, I'm 17, and now I'm a junior in high school. I love my boyfriend a lot. When I got pregnant, well . . . I didn't mean for it to happen, but it just did. I considered abortion and adoption . . . but . . . in the final decision . . . I couldn't do it. My mom and step-dad were real real angry at first. It took them about a month before they would talk about my pregnancy without either crying or screaming. That might have been the worst part of it. I felt like I disappointed my parents," Laura describes with tears in her eyes. "After my mom came around, she tried to convince me to give my baby up for adoption. We checked into all of the services and agencies . . . together. I decided that I couldn't do that, and when I decided, she just hugged me and said that I had a long road ahead, but that she would be there for me. I think that was a real hard time for her."

"I wanted her to go to college. I wanted her to be successful and happy. I guess my ideas of happy and successful weren't being a mom at 17," Alice, Laura's mom, said as she came in from the kitchen with a bottle for her grandson. She handed it to Laura and stroked her grandson's head at the same time with a loving smile on her face. "It was a very tough time for our family. My husband and I, Laura's step-father, we didn't sleep much for a long time, and the tension around this house was terrible. We thought that this pregnancy, and her becoming a mother would be the end of her. We couldn't see beyond the fact that it appeared that she ruined her life by having a baby at 17," Alice went on to say, "It just didn't seem possible that my daughter was going to be a mother."

Charlie: A Teen Dad

"I really wanted to go out with Laura. She was pretty and she was cute and she was so talented. When she was up on the stage in the high school play, I couldn't take my eyes off of her. I finally got up enough nerve to ask her out," Charlie said. Charlie is a tall, lanky, 17-year-old junior as well, a basketball player, and a class clown. "We went out. We spent all of our free time together. She came to watch me practice and play, and I went to her rehearsals and every performance. We had a group of friends that we would hang out with on the weekends. We don't hang out with them anymore," Charlie said as his eyes looked down at his shoes.

"I didn't know she was pregnant at first. She was tired and sick to her stomach at first. I just guessed it was nerves with the musical and all. Finally one day she sat across from me at lunch and told me. I was shocked. I know she said some things after she told me, but I don't remember what they were. I don't remember much about that afternoon at all," Charlie remembers. "I went through the rest of the day; I guess I was kinda numb."

"I didn't tell my mom. When she did find out she blew a gasket. She kept saying '. . . don't be like your father . . . take care of your responsibility' over and over. She cried a lot and bought a car seat for the baby. When Laura came over, she hugged her tight and cried. I think she felt connected to her," Charlie said as he looks across the room at a picture of his son. "I'm a dad. I'm 17 and I'm a dad. I was there when he was born. It was so incredible. Everyone says he looks like me and when you hold up our baby pictures together we look alike."

A Committed Couple

They sit together on the couch in her parents' living room. Their son is asleep in Laura's room in a crib next to her bed. They have just come home from school, picked up the baby from the sitter and put him down for a quick nap.

"I stayed in school until a week before he was born. I couldn't fit in the desks by then, and it was hard to walk up and down the stairs. I was in labor for 30 hours . . . it seemed like forever," Laura talked quietly as she yawned. "Sorry about that. I didn't sleep much last night." Charlie puts his arm around her.

"I asked her to marry me when I had a chance to think about it," Charlie explains, "but she said no. She said if we get married, let's do it because we want to, not because we have to. I was sort of relieved when she said that. I love her, but I didn't know if I was ready to get married. I just know that I needed to ask her."

Laura explains, "I love Charlie . . . but I didn't want to tie him to this and then he'd probably hate me and the baby. Our parents have worked together to help us make this all work. I live here at home with my mom and step-dad. They want me to finish high school, so they are paying for daycare and the extras for the baby so I don't have to work right now. I'm so lucky in that way, I know some girls are working and going to school and taking care of a baby. That is so much to do. My parents always promised that they'd pay for me to got to college too. I don't know what will happen there, but I'm lucky that they are supportive of me and of Charlie."

"I work after school and on Saturdays. I give Laura $100.00 a month for the baby. That helps with diapers and formula and other stuff. I will finish high school too, I promised my mom that I would and that I would always take care of my son," Charlie says as he grabs Laura's hand.

A Special Family of Three

"We have different friends now. Some of our old friends don't understand that I can't come out on a Wednesday night at the spur of the moment. They think it is easy to be a mom, and that my parents will help whenever. Well, it's not true. I miss out on a lot of school stuff, and really, anymore, it isn't all that important. It's not like playing house. He depends on me for everything, and I just can't go out if I want to. I guess I miss that the most. When I do go out, I have to bundle up the baby and go."

"Her folks let me come and spend as much time with them as I can. The only thing is that we can't let our grades slip. We promised, and I suppose that this is the first thing that we can teach our son. We do homework together, I give him a bath a couple of times a week, and sometimes I take him to my house . . . just him and me," Charlie explains. "It gives Laura some time to get some sleep. In the summer I will work full-time so that I can help with other things for him as well. And I want to take Laura and the baby to visit my grandparents, and that all costs a lot of money."

The baby cries from the other room. Charlie gets up and motions that he'll do it. "He's great with him. I know that we didn't plan this, and when I read about other single teen parents, we have it pretty easy. I feel alone in this, I'm single and I didn't marry Charlie, and that is my choice. I've met some other moms who are in high school, and we talk once in a while. It is nice to know that there [are] other moms out there who feel and think about the same things that I do." Charlie walks in the room with the baby. "Look . . . aren't they special," Laura says as Charlie sits next to her.

They are special. As a family, they sit together on the couch with their son on his dad's lap. Just 17, they have found a way to make it work as single teen parents. "We don't know what the future holds right now. I just want to finish high school, then we'll see what happens," Laura says.

"Me too," adds Charlie. "I just know that life is different now, and that it isn't so bad," he winks as he says that and he kisses his son.

ORGANIZATIONS TO CONTACT

The editors have compiled the following list of organizations concerned with the issues presented in this book. The descriptions are derived from materials provided by the organizations. All have publications or information available for interested readers. The list was compiled on the date of publication of the present volume; the information provided here may change. Be aware that many organizations take several weeks or longer to respond to inquiries, so allow as much time as possible.

Advocates for Youth
1025 Vermont Ave. NW, Suite 200, Washington, DC 20005
(202) 347-5700 • fax: (202) 347-2263
e-mail: info@advocatesforyouth.org • website: www.advocatesforyouth.org

Advocates for Youth's focus is on preventing pregnancy and sexually transmitted diseases (STDs) among young people. The organization's Rights, Respect, and Responsibility Campaign, initiated in 2001, helps young people and adults work together to protect the sexual health of all adolescents. Through its specialized clearinghouses on sexuality education, teen pregnancy and HIV/STD prevention, school condom availability, peer education, school-based health centers, and adolescent reproductive health initiatives, the organization provides up-to-date information to educators, students, policy makers, and healthcare providers. Its numerous publications include the newsletters *Transitions* and *Advocates Alert* and the pamphlets *America's Least Wanted: Sexually Transmitted Diseases, Advice from Teens on Buying Condoms,* and *I Think I Might Be Lesbian: Now What Do I Do?*

Alan Guttmacher Institute (AGI)
120 Wall St., New York, NY 10005
(212) 248-1111 • fax: (212) 248-1951
e-mail: info@agi-usa.org • website: www.agi-usa.org

AGI works to protect and expand the reproductive choices of all women and men worldwide. The institute strives to ensure people's access to the information and services they need to exercise their rights and responsibilities concerning sexual activity, reproduction, and family planning. It conducts domestic and international projects designed to foster reproductive health, effective prevention of unintended pregnancy, the right to abortion, and societal support for parenting. Among the institute's publications are the reports "Sex and America's Teenagers" and "Why Is Teenage Pregnancy Declining? The Roles of Abstinence, Sexual Activity, and Contraceptive Use," the bimonthly periodical *Family Planning Perspectives,* and the quarterly periodical *International Family Planning Perspectives.*

American Social Health Association (ASHA)
PO Box 13827, Research Triangle Park, NC 27709
(919) 361-8400 • fax: (919) 361-8425
e-mail: phidra@ashastd.org • website: www.ashastd.org

A public health advocacy organization, ASHA works to raise awareness about sexually transmitted diseases (STDs) and to eliminate their spread and harmful consequences. The association provides current and medically sound information about the transmission, prevention, and treatment of sexually transmitted diseases. Its publications include the quarterly newsletters *The Helper* (about herpes) and *HPV News* (about human papillomavirus), the book *Managing Herpes: How to Live and Love with a Chronic STD*, and the booklets *Understanding Herpes* and *HPV in Perspective: A Patient Guide*.

Campaign for Our Children (CFOC)
120 W. Fayette St., Suite 1200, Baltimore, MD 21201
(410) 576-9015
website: www.cfoc.org

CFOC uses mass media advertising, media relations, school programs, and public health outlets to promote abstinence to adolescents. The organization produces educational videos, lesson plans, posters, television and radio ads, billboards, and brochures in English and Spanish. Among its publications are the brochure *Talking the Talk* and the educational sets "Abstinence Makes the Heart Grow Fonder" and "You Play, You Pay."

Child Welfare League of America (CWLA)
440 First St. NW, Third Floor, Washington, DC 20001-2085
(202) 638-2952 • fax: (202) 638-4004
e-mail: webweaver@cwla.org • website: www.cwla.org

CWLA develops and promotes policies and programs designed to protect America's children and strengthen America's families. Its member agencies provide a variety of services, such as child protection, kinship care, family foster care, adoption, and programs for pregnant and parenting teenagers. The league's publications include *First Talk: A Teen Pregnancy Prevention Dialogue Among Latinos, Facing Teenage Pregnancy: A Handbook for the Pregnant Teen, Welfare Reform and Abstinence Education,* and *Adolescent Sexuality, Pregnancy, and Parenting: Selected Readings*.

Coalition for Positive Sexuality (CPS)
PO Box 77212, Washington, DC 20013-7212
(773) 604-1654
website: www.positive.org

A grassroots volunteer group, CPS was formed by high school students to provide teens with sex-positive and safe sex information and to facilitate dialogue on condom availability and sex education. The CPS booklet *Just Say Yes*—written by teens for teens and available in English and in Spanish—addresses many issues concerning teen sexuality, including homosexuality, birth control, and sexually transmitted diseases.

ETR Associates
PO Box 1830, Santa Cruz, CA 95061-1830
(831) 438-4060
website: www.etr.org

ETR Associates provides leadership, educational resources, training, and research in health promotion with an emphasis on sexuality and health education. The organization publishes a wide variety of health education resources, including books, flip charts, curricula, the videotapes *First Things First: Teenage Relationships* and *Birth Control for Teens,* and the pamphlets *101 Ways to Make Love Without Doin' It, Abstinence 101,* and *It Only Takes a Minute: Condoms.* It also maintains the online Resource Center for Adolescent Pregnancy Prevention (www.etr.org/recapp), which provides practical, up-to-date tools and information to help teachers and health educators reduce sexual risk-taking behaviors in teens.

Family Research Council
801 G St. NW, Washington, DC 20001
(202) 393-2100 • fax: (202) 393-2134
e-mail: corrdept@frc.org • website: www.frc.org

The council seeks to promote and protect the interests of the traditional family. It focuses on issues such as abstinence and sex education, adolescent pregnancy, and community supports for single parents. Among the council's numerous publications are the papers "Revolt of the Virgins," "Abstinence: The New Sexual Revolution," and "Abstinence Programs Show Promise in Reducing Sexual Activity and Pregnancy Among Teens."

Gay, Lesbian and Straight Education Network (GLSEN)
121 West 27th St., Suite 804, New York, NY 10001-6207
(212) 727-0135 • fax: (212) 727-0254
e-mail: glsen@glsen.org • website: www.glsen.org

GLSEN works to combat anti-gay bias and hate-motivated violence in schools through education. In addition to serving as a community resource for accurate information about the lesbian, gay, bisexual, and transgendered community, the organization provides relevant educational and curricular materials to public schools. Through its Student Pride project, GLSEN helps high school students form and maintain Gay-Straight Alliances. The organization's resources include the curriculum guide *Lesbian, Gay, Bisexual, and Transgender Rights: A Human Rights Perspective* and the videotapes *I Just Want to Say* and *Outside the Lines: The World of the Gay Athlete*.

National Minority AIDS Council (NMAC)
1931 13th St. NW, Washington, DC 20009
(202) 483-6622 • fax: (202) 483-1135
e-mail: info@nmac.org • website: www.nmac.org

NMAC is dedicated to developing leadership within communities of color to confront HIV/AIDS and related issues. The council also monitors and addresses HIV/AIDS legislation, promotes minority community–based organizations and planning groups, and serves as an advocate for people of color living with HIV/AIDS. Its publications include a series of reference manuals, brochures, and fact sheets. In addition, NMAC publishes three newsletters: *Treatment Alert*, which focuses on research and treatment advocacy, *Connections*, which provides technical assistance to community organizations, and *Update*, which addresses public policy issues.

National Youth Advocacy Coalition (NYAC)
1638 R St. NW, Suite 300, Washington, DC 20009
(202) 319-7596 • fax: (202) 319-7365
e-mail: nyac@nyacyouth.org • website: www.nyacyouth.org

NYAC's mission is to act as an advocate for lesbian, gay, bisexual, and transgender (LGBT) teens, working to ensure their well-being and to end discrimination against them. It maintains the Bridges Project, a clearinghouse that provides information, referrals, and technical assistance in regard to coalition building, volunteer programs, peer counseling, and other related areas of interest. NYAC publishes *Crossroads* magazine and a series of information packets devoted to specific issues of concern to LGBT youth.

Sex Education Coalition

PO Box 341751, Bethesda, MD 20827-1751
fax: (810) 222-1910
e-mail: webmaster@SexEdCoalition.org • website: www.sexedcoalition.org

The coalition's purpose is to promote sexual health based upon scientifically sound principles of health promotion and educational research. It is composed of educators, health care professionals, trainers, and legislators dedicated to providing the public with up-to-date information concerning comprehensive sexuality education. Through its website, the coalition offers a variety of materials and resources about sexuality education, as well as a forum for discussion.

Sexuality Information and Education Council of the United States (SIECUS)

130 W. 42nd St., Suite 350, New York, NY 10036-7802
(212) 819-9770 • fax: (212) 819-9776
e-mail: siecus@siecus.org • website: www.siecus.org

SIECUS promotes comprehensive education about sexuality and advocates the right of individuals to make responsible sexual choices. The council maintains the Mary S. Calderone Library, which offers resource materials on all aspects of human sexuality. SIECUS publishes and distributes diverse resources, including pamphlets, booklets, annotated bibliographies, the fact sheets "Adolescence and Abstinence" and "Teen Pregnancy," the bimonthly journal *SIECUS Report*, and the biweekly bulletin *SHOPTalk*.

BIBLIOGRAPHY

Books

Michael W. Adler   *ABC of Sexually Transmitted Diseases.* Chicago, IL: Login Brothers, 1999.

Eleanor Ayer   *It's Okay to Say No: Choosing Sexual Abstinence.* New York: Rosen, 1997.

Michael J. Basso   *The Underground Guide to Teenage Sexuality: An Essential Handbook for Today's Teens and Parents.* Minneapolis, MN: Fairview Press, 1997.

Peter S. Bearman et al.   *Peer Potential: Making the Most of How Teens Influence Each Other.* Washington, DC: National Campaign to Prevent Teen Pregnancy, 1999.

Ruth Bell   *Changing Bodies, Changing Lives: A Book for Teens on Sex and Relationships.* New York: Times Books, 1998.

Jeanne Blake   *Risky Times: How To Be AIDS-Smart and Stay Healthy.* New York: Workman, 1990.

Janet Bode   *Heartbreak and Roses: Real Life Stories of Troubled Love.* Danbury, CT: Franklin Watts, 2000.

Janet Bode   *Kids Still Having Kids: Talking About Teen Pregnancy.* Danbury, CT: Franklin Watts, 1999.

Barbara Christie-Dever   *AIDS: What Teens Need to Know.* Santa Barbara, CA: Learning Works, 1996.

Columbia University's Health Education Program   *The "Go Ask Alice" Book of Answers: A Guide to Good Physical, Sexual, and Emotional Health.* New York: Owl Books, 1998.

Paula Edelson   *Teenage Pregnancy.* New York: Facts On File, 1998.

Julie K. Endersbe   *Homosexuality: What Does it Mean?* Mankato, MN: Capstone Press/LifeMatters, 2000.

Julie K. Endersbe   *Sexual Readiness: When Is it Right?* Mankato, MN: Capstone Press/LifeMatters, 2000.

Julie K. Endersbe   *Sexually Transmitted Diseases: How Are They Prevented?* Mankato, MN: Capstone Press/LifeMatters, 2000.

Gilbert Herdt   *Children of Horizons: How Gay and Lesbian Teens Are Leading a New Way Out of the Closet.* Boston, MA: Beacon Press, 1996.

John Hutchins, Tamara Kreinin, Anne Brown Rodgers, and Susan Kuhn, eds.   *Get Organized: A Guide to Preventing Teen Pregnancy.* Washington, DC: National Campaign to Prevent Teen Pregnancy, 1999.

Kimberly Kirberger   *On Relationships: A Book for Teenagers.* Deerfield Beach, FL: Health Communications, 1999.

| James E. Lieberman and Karen Lieberman Troccoli | *Like it Is: A Teen Sex Guide.* Jefferson, NC: McFarland, 1998. |

James E. Lieberman and Karen Lieberman Troccoli — *Like it Is: A Teen Sex Guide.* Jefferson, NC: McFarland, 1998.

Susan Lieberman and Nathalie A. Bartle — *Venus in Blue Jeans: Why Mothers and Daughters Need to Talk About Sex.* New York: Dell Books, 1999.

Jeanne Warren Lindsey — *Teenage Couples: Expectations and Reality: Teen Views on Living Together, Roles, Work, Jealousy, and Partner Abuse.* Buena Park, CA: Morning Glory Press, 1996.

Bronwyn Mayden, Wendy Castro, and Megan Annitto — *First Talk: A Teen Pregnancy Prevention Dialogue Among Latinos.* Washington, DC: Child Welfare League of America, 1999.

Kathy McCoy and Charles Wibbelsman — *The Teenage Body Book.* New York: Perigee, 1999.

Don Nardo — *Teen Sex.* San Diego, CA: Lucent Press, 1996.

National Campaign to Prevent Teen Pregnancy Staff, ed. — *Voices Carry: Teens Speak Out on Sex and Teen Pregnancy.* Washington, DC: National Campaign to Prevent Teen Pregnancy, 2000.

Jeffrey A. Nevid — *Choices: Sex in the Age of STDs.* Needham Heights, MA: Allyn and Bacon, 1997.

Judith Peacock — *Birth Control and Protection: Choices for Teens.* Mankato, MN: Capstone Press, 2000.

Susan Browning Pogany — *Sex Smart: 501 Reasons to Hold Off on Sex.* Minneapolis, MN: Fairview Press, 1998.

Rachel Pollack — *Journey Out: A Guide for Lesbian, Gay, and Bisexual Teens.* Topeka, KS: Econo-Clad Books, 1999.

Tara Roberts and Malik Yusek — *Am I the Last Virgin? African American Reflections on Sex and Love.* New York: Aladdin, 1996.

Sabrina Solin — *The Seventeen Guide to Sex and Your Body.* New York: Simon and Schuster, 1996.

Robert Starr — *AIDS: Why Should I Care? Teens Across America Speak Out.* Los Angeles, CA: PTAAA Press, 1999.

Margi Trapani — *Listen Up! Teenage Mothers Speak Out.* New York: Rosen, 1997.

Margi Trapani — *Reality Check: Teenage Fathers Speak Out.* New York: Rosen, 1999.

Jessica Vitkus, Marjorie Ingall, and Jessica Weeks — *Smart Sex.* New York: Pocket Books, 1998.

Renée T. White — *Putting Risk in Perspective: Black Teenage Lives in the Era of AIDS.* Lanham, MD: Rowman and Littlefield, 1999.

Samuel G. Woods — *Everything You Need to Know About STD: Sexually Transmitted Disease.* New York: Rosen, 2000.

Youth Communication — *Starting with "I": Personal Essays by Teenagers.* New York: Persea Books, 1997.

Periodicals

Link Byfield	"The Teen Sex Solution," *Alberta Report,* October 11, 1999. Available from 17327-106A Ave., Edmonton, AB T5S 1M7 Canada.
John Cloud	"Out, Proud and Very Young," *Time,* December 8, 1997.
Amy Dickinson	"Teenage Sex: Pregnancy Is Down Among Teens, but They're Still Having Sex Too Soon. What's a Parent to Do?" *Time,* November 8, 1999.
Kendra E. Fish	"Waiting for the Results of an AIDS Test Can Be a Soul-Searching Experience," *Rocky Mountain Collegian,* November 12, 1999. Available from Colorado State University, Lory Student Center, Box 13, Fort Collins, CO 80523-0001.
Mary Guiden	"Not Your Average Teen Mom," *State Legislatures,* February 2000. Available from National Conference of State Legislatures, 1560 Broadway, Suite 700, Denver, CO 80202-5140.
Debra W. Haffner	"Message from the President: Sexuality Issues 2010," *SIECUS Report,* New York, December 1999/January 2000.
Dan Hurley	"The Truth About Teens and Sex," *Family Circle,* October 5, 1999.
James Jaccard	"Parent-Teen Communication About Premarital Sex: Factors Associated with the Extent of Communication," *Journal of Adolescent Research,* March 2000. Available from Sage Publications, 2455 Teller Rd., Thousand Oaks, CA 91326-2218.
Sandra Kallio	"School Life Tough for Gay Teens: Vulnerable Students Desperate for Support," *Wisconsin State Journal,* January 25, 2000. Available at www.wisconsinstatejournal.com.
Lillian Lee Kim	"Teens Lack Information About Sex," *Atlanta Journal-Constitution,* October 29, 1999. Available at www.ajc.com.
Douglas Kirby	"Reflections on Two Decades of Research on Teen Sexual Behavior and Pregnancy," *Journal of School Health,* March 1999. Available from the American School Health Association, PO Box 708, 7263 State Rte. 43, Kent, OH 44240-0013.
Carolyn Mackler	"Sex Ed: How Do We Score?" *Ms.,* August/September 1999.
Candy McCrary	"You Just Had Unprotected Sex with Your Boyfriend," *Virginian-Pilot,* February 25, 2000. Available from 150 W. Brambleton Ave., Norfolk, VA 23510-2075.
Minneapolis Star Tribune	"Teen Pregnancy Rate Plummets," April 29, 1999. Available at www.startribune.com.

Richard Nadler   "Birds, Bees, and ABC's," *National Review,* September
                          13, 1999.

Gerald S. Oettinger   "The Effects of Sex Education on Teen Sexual Activity
                          and Teen Pregnancy," *Journal of Political Economy,* June
                          1999.

John O'Neil   "Of Sex, Smarts and the Teenage Mind," *New York
                          Times,* March 7, 2000.

People Weekly   "Revisiting 'The Baby Trap,'" October 11, 1999.

Isabel V. Sawhill   "Welfare Reform and Reducing Teen Pregnancy,"
                          Public Interest, Winter 2000.

INDEX